PASSWORD GENERATOR
FOR
TEN-SIDED DICE

FEATURING TEN THOUSAND NOUNS

PASSWORD GENERATOR
FOR
TEN-SIDED DICE

FEATURING TEN THOUSAND NOUNS

WWW.PASSWORDGENERATORDICE.COM

ISBN: 1985202980
ISBN-13: 978-1985202986

INSTRUCTIONS

To generate a password using this password generator for ten-sided dice, you need two ten-sided dice: one labeled 0 to 9, and the other labeled 00 to 90. You can get these from your local games shop or from www.passwordgeneratordice.com.

Roll the dice and add the numbers together. Turn to that page. On that page there are a hundred nouns numbered from 0 to 99. Roll the dice again and add the numbers together to see which of those nouns you will include in your password. For example, if you roll a 2 and a 10 on your first roll, you would turn to page 12. Then if you roll an 8 and a 40, you would include the noun numbered 48, "Software."

If you include only one noun in your password, there is a 1 in 10 thousand chance that it will be guessed on the first try. This is inadequate for most security applications. So, repeat the process in the previous paragraph to get at least three more nouns to include in your password. Continuing the previous example, your password might be "SoftwareBucketStarAnthropology." With four nouns, there is only a 1 in 10 quadrillion chance that it will be guessed on the first try.

0. Starter	34. Betrayal	68. Seabed
1. Iodine	35. Colleague	69. Stardust
2. Vestry	36. Split	70. Hiding
3. Banter	37. Winch	71. Kettledrum
4. Oblong	38. Noisemaker	72. Firecracker
5. Tower	39. Odds	73. Thoughtlessness
6. Ballerina	40. Captor	74. Shaver
7. Seer	41. Cheep	75. Salsa
8. Prefix	42. Albino	76. Thriller
9. Sentience	43. Tolerance	77. Blotch
10. Landing	44. Throng	78. Longboat
11. Streetcar	45. Yard	79. Asset
12. Ceremony	46. Mysticism	80. Henchman
13. Composer	47. Cowherd	81. Construction
14. Perfume	48. Tradesman	82. Husband
15. Generic	49. Red	83. Snail
16. Heart	50. Pasta	84. Eccentricity
17. Monster	51. Saccharine	85. Doe
18. Shore	52. Crinkle	86. Seeing
19. Ice	53. Vicinity	87. Mammoth
20. Toothpick	54. Smock	88. Publisher
21. Houseguest	55. Muscle	89. Hairbrush
22. Readiness	56. Laundry	90. Irrelevance
23. Confinement	57. Phlox	91. Bed
24. Steward	58. Verger	92. Hunter
25. Vegetation	59. Drummer	93. Scenario
26. Bun	60. Throw	94. Cornstarch
27. Artiste	61. Keepsake	95. Delinquency
28. Eagerness	62. Act	96. Furnishings
29. Dormouse	63. Railway	97. Aftermath
30. Monument	64. Proletariat	98. Oxygen
31. Trim	65. Disbandment	99. Slat
32. Crew	66. Salesperson	
33. Friary	67. Galleon	

0. Cornet
1. Landfall
2. Interference
3. Lap
4. Plaintiff
5. Glory
6. Storybook
7. Doily
8. Omnibus
9. Afterthought
10. Arbor
11. Block
12. Prefect
13. Ultrasound
14. Floodlight
15. Bucket
16. Percentage
17. Renovation
18. Email
19. Labor
20. Preposition
21. Office
22. Leverage
23. Errand
24. Pique
25. Fingerprint
26. Contemporary
27. Misogynist
28. Chops
29. Wit
30. Degeneration
31. Extraction
32. Haze
33. Carelessness
34. Breakthrough
35. Redemption
36. Wholesale
37. Skewer
38. Bassoon
39. Nightmare
40. Soprano
41. Prioress
42. Humanitarian
43. Dam
44. Boom
45. Suavity
46. Bulge
47. Lore
48. Ionosphere
49. Propaganda
50. Plume
51. Puppet
52. Hardwood
53. Flat
54. Swoop
55. Ihram
56. Hairpin
57. Voice
58. Cockatoo
59. Drowsiness
60. Hugeness
61. Literacy
62. Ghastliness
63. Monarch
64. Return
65. Archery
66. Stereotype
67. Corrosive
68. Ukulele
69. Wok
70. Dumbness
71. Tutu
72. Parachute
73. Produce
74. Value
75. Divan
76. Lobby
77. Serial
78. Seconds
79. Cowardice
80. Activity
81. Womanhood
82. Fox
83. Revelation
84. Graph
85. Mechanics
86. Saber
87. Telepathy
88. Allocation
89. Font
90. Trajectory
91. Gust
92. Savvy
93. Brawl
94. Prophetess
95. Table
96. Softball
97. Sneer
98. Consumer
99. Evocation

0. Filly	34. Hailstorm	68. Prong
1. Glitch	35. Figurine	69. Lesson
2. Doll	36. Dividers	70. Mammal
3. Pastel	37. Ancestor	71. Hamlet
4. Burrow	38. Distillation	72. Quart
5. Insured	39. Mortar	73. Fifty
6. Antelope	40. Joy	74. Jetsam
7. Map	41. Privacy	75. Misandrist
8. Moss	42. Pilferer	76. Subversion
9. Immodesty	43. Sleuth	77. Eel
10. Bank	44. Annex	78. Study
11. Trend	45. Flange	79. Fluorescence
12. Dream	46. Delight	80. Toe
13. Downstairs	47. Rim	81. Lacquer
14. Sugar	48. Mockery	82. Setting
15. Robber	49. Cocoon	83. Yak
16. Grotto	50. Historian	84. Byte
17. Antipathy	51. Betrothal	85. Tonnage
18. Soliloquy	52. Sarong	86. Scarcity
19. Treatment	53. Buffer	87. Probate
20. Shunpike	54. Padding	88. Silver
21. Format	55. Brass	89. Savings
22. Logarithm	56. Turkey	90. Mourning
23. Individuality	57. Philosopher	91. Race
24. Refinery	58. Cottage	92. Vise
25. Schoolroom	59. Aim	93. Brill
26. Woodland	60. Restaurant	94. Registration
27. Uproar	61. Spout	95. Indigene
28. Seventeenth	62. Reactionary	96. Lane
29. Nutrition	63. Farfel	97. Nightingale
30. Railing	64. Typhoon	98. Heyday
31. Crescendo	65. Drudgery	99. Cradle
32. Billfold	66. Fraud	
33. Consultant	67. Wader	

0. Temptation	34. Slope	68. Subscription
1. Loganberry	35. Virility	69. Vortex
2. Bound	36. Firefly	70. Norm
3. Alibi	37. Protocol	71. Sellout
4. Demise	38. Prophet	72. Treasury
5. Signpost	39. Sender	73. Standstill
6. Mayor	40. Toxicology	74. Net
7. Contrition	41. Sightseer	75. Text
8. Cassette	42. Camera	76. Hoe
9. Shellfish	43. Glue	77. Puma
10. Informality	44. Improbability	78. Phosphorous
11. Sportsmanship	45. Nameplate	79. Dregs
12. Documentary	46. Shears	80. Reading
13. Dynasty	47. Complacence	81. Surrey
14. Accomplice	48. Compost	82. Temple
15. Tune	49. Flounce	83. Valance
16. Thermodynamics	50. Heartbreaker	84. Bygones
17. Creditor	51. Audience	85. Vacuum
18. Flirt	52. Bush	86. Savanna
19. Wildcat	53. Anniversary	87. Punctuality
20. Scandal	54. Trawler	88. Dodge
21. Baboon	55. Vicar	89. Protestation
22. Ritual	56. Masquerade	90. River
23. Grapefruit	57. Superhero	91. Mimic
24. Partition	58. City	92. Cask
25. Agitation	59. Transcript	93. Unity
26. Lifestyle	60. Participant	94. Safekeeping
27. Story	61. Roast	95. Weakness
28. Brood	62. Accompanist	96. Acquittal
29. Deferment	63. Nudist	97. Tussle
30. Levee	64. Croupier	98. Dupe
31. Expulsion	65. Mend	99. Cackle
32. Shelving	66. Tartan	
33. Futon	67. Chessmen	

0. Taxidermy
1. Bid
2. Parasol
3. Reappearance
4. Innuendo
5. Cellphone
6. Optimism
7. Fume
8. Rosette
9. Crag
10. Suffrage
11. Salmon
12. Terrain
13. Disguise
14. Catacomb
15. Conclave
16. Season
17. Route
18. Zero
19. Shave
20. Prognosis
21. Enrapture
22. Putty
23. Fajita
24. Commendation
25. Dome
26. Tact
27. Confederate
28. Purveyor
29. Timer
30. Crossbow
31. Worker
32. Promontory
33. Trapeze
34. Pouch
35. Comforter
36. Reprimand
37. Silencer
38. Leakage
39. Sibyl
40. Cloud
41. Giddiness
42. Centennial
43. Pottage
44. Milligram
45. Dune
46. Forte
47. Fauna
48. Locomotive
49. Pigtail
50. Aisle
51. Pin
52. Trot
53. Marten
54. Disability
55. Excavation
56. Origin
57. Excess
58. File
59. Moral
60. Ping
61. Hunt
62. Overcoat
63. Scampi
64. Talon
65. Cost
66. Notice
67. Deputy
68. Elevator
69. Exhibit
70. Swim
71. Harebell
72. Tresses
73. Excuse
74. Player
75. Staple
76. Vespers
77. Outfit
78. Hake
79. Underbrush
80. Geometry
81. Surfing
82. Briefcase
83. Analog
84. Method
85. Priesthood
86. Herd
87. Phalanx
88. Learner
89. Weevil
90. Summer
91. Bag
92. Paleontologist
93. Trifle
94. Translator
95. Gram
96. Work
97. Sturgeon
98. Orchard
99. Nanometer

0. Eddy	34. Bang	68. Pence
1. Antithesis	35. Carnivore	69. Evaluation
2. Cavalier	36. Limp	70. Curse
3. Bunk	37. Adversity	71. Gingham
4. Boulevard	38. Tread	72. Shutout
5. Nicety	39. Achievement	73. Anticipation
6. Intimation	40. Jelly	74. Prospective
7. Bilberry	41. Contraption	75. Richness
8. Cousin	42. Irritation	76. Wave
9. Equilibrium	43. Spillover	77. Stain
10. Keyhole	44. Saffron	78. Sustenance
11. Perplexity	45. Mural	79. Bird
12. Dentist	46. Glen	80. Marmalade
13. Drone	47. Vizier	81. Xylophone
14. Backboard	48. Commencement	82. Burnish
15. Remember	49. Bane	83. Providence
16. Republican	50. Chimney	84. Benchmark
17. Barrage	51. Adequate	85. Additive
18. Tabloid	52. Plodder	86. Eavesdropper
19. Junk	53. Reverence	87. Healthcare
20. Beau	54. Boredom	88. Subordinate
21. Rambler	55. Opposition	89. Sensuality
22. Swami	56. Skyscraper	90. Navel
23. Slingshot	57. Patience	91. Inanity
24. Selfishness	58. Bonus	92. Allegory
25. Call	59. Sasquatch	93. Cue
26. Integrity	60. Drover	94. Carcass
27. Buck	61. Priming	95. Minx
28. Side	62. Cream	96. Accessory
29. Pathology	63. Spectacle	97. Resource
30. Tannery	64. Restriction	98. Doggerel
31. Swallow	65. Blonde	99. Powwow
32. Onlooker	66. Apparel	
33. Allowance	67. Ewe	

0. Chimes	34. Gallop	68. Scarf
1. Ringleader	35. Bludgeon	69. Anarchist
2. Hygiene	36. Spawn	70. Vitality
3. Artist	37. Tress	71. Pageant
4. Whistle	38. Dory	72. Daily
5. Woof	39. Bison	73. Nonexistence
6. Sensibility	40. Count	74. Oarsman
7. Solemnity	41. Halter	75. Directory
8. Steel	42. Sniper	76. Etymology
9. Brush	43. Crust	77. Sanctum
10. Trinket	44. Mutter	78. Macaw
11. Intension	45. Screensaver	79. Fission
12. Newlywed	46. Stud	80. Virulence
13. Rage	47. Niece	81. Concoction
14. Speculator	48. Scooter	82. Sherry
15. Peerage	49. Illegality	83. Humpback
16. Intricacy	50. Grape	84. Hajj
17. Oatcake	51. Seersucker	85. Atmosphere
18. Contradiction	52. Hypnotism	86. Polka
19. Volition	53. Cleverness	87. Cloak
20. Freshener	54. Biscuit	88. Remembrance
21. Variant	55. Gloss	89. Tournament
22. Lexicon	56. Pickpocket	90. Riddle
23. Wicker	57. Secret	91. Entrant
24. Blank	58. Constancy	92. Complement
25. Sleeper	59. Bye	93. Prologue
26. Suffragist	60. Toothache	94. Prayer
27. Hyena	61. Spinning	95. Hooligan
28. Shimmy	62. Leprechaun	96. Buckskin
29. Toboggan	63. Handhold	97. Child
30. Patchwork	64. Plenitude	98. Consecration
31. Hiss	65. Instability	99. Sentimentality
32. Sweet	66. Lentil	
33. Gill	67. Mortality	

0. Abstention
1. Adult
2. Knight
3. Attention
4. Sloop
5. Immobility
6. Scramble
7. Stable
8. Tempo
9. Proclamation
10. Indecision
11. Deliberation
12. Close
13. Pore
14. Safety
15. Insertion
16. Nag
17. Witchcraft
18. Grace
19. Beholder
20. Indulgence
21. Network
22. Colon
23. Penknife
24. Device
25. Development
26. Collision
27. Hospice
28. Paste
29. Legality
30. Courtesy
31. Assay
32. Purification
33. Amalgam
34. Chili
35. Enchantress
36. Tomb
37. Commiseration
38. Nightshirt
39. Coastline
40. Highland
41. Crab
42. Gem
43. Toiler
44. Handlebar
45. Quadrant
46. Agitator
47. Pedigree
48. Doorway
49. Dulcimer
50. Stroke
51. Kamik
52. Suture
53. Participle
54. Informer
55. Caribou
56. Brine
57. Mullet
58. Narcotic
59. Workmanship
60. Sum
61. Columnist
62. Comma
63. Almanac
64. Urgency
65. Swerve
66. Feeler
67. Massacre
68. Promotion
69. Derivative
70. Headstone
71. Club
72. Competence
73. Tactician
74. Slouch
75. Gentleness
76. Function
77. Datum
78. Frond
79. Node
80. Role
81. Isolation
82. Quotient
83. Periscope
84. Packaging
85. Vowel
86. Tie
87. Anchorage
88. Framework
89. Boomerang
90. Extirpation
91. Belt
92. Shaman
93. Spindle
94. Fee
95. Aerosol
96. Promiscuity
97. Wrongdoer
98. Prowler
99. Notation

0. Uranium	34. Cacophony	68. Euphemism
1. Pincers	35. Lowing	69. Enjoyment
2. Prestige	36. Cardinal	70. Arcade
3. Data	37. Glibness	71. Epitaph
4. Picnic	38. Idiosyncrasy	72. Inclusion
5. Apology	39. Intifada	73. Vacancy
6. Rebirth	40. Pallet	74. Auxiliary
7. Bray	41. Correspondent	75. Spectacles
8. Instrument	42. Obedience	76. Sailboard
9. Illumination	43. Smile	77. Sixth
10. Announcer	44. Bowling	78. Fire
11. Perk	45. Ladybug	79. Nirvana
12. Flatbread	46. Squeezebox	80. Architecture
13. Means	47. Terminology	81. Physiology
14. Limb	48. Semicircle	82. Cant
15. Humor	49. Daydream	83. Loyalty
16. Era	50. Outrage	84. Badminton
17. Elegance	51. Grade	85. Metaphysics
18. Abstainer	52. Sailboat	86. Speckle
19. Rubble	53. Orchestration	87. Oval
20. Dawn	54. Swipe	88. Croissant
21. Weight	55. Cartoon	89. Peseta
22. Observance	56. Acquaintance	90. Inquisitor
23. Clone	57. Frigidity	91. Granddaughter
24. Proponent	58. Turret	92. Provocation
25. Heist	59. Publicity	93. Faith
26. Brag	60. Effluence	94. Splurge
27. Vinyl	61. Hippies	95. Mettle
28. Recorder	62. Sling	96. Rapport
29. Party	63. Hob	97. Razorblade
30. Occupation	64. Handicap	98. Jib
31. Callousness	65. Scribe	99. Booty
32. Regent	66. Polythene	
33. Spoke	67. Mystery	

0. Horticulture
1. Racism
2. Democrat
3. Legislator
4. Underwear
5. Injection
6. Musical
7. Forage
8. Gluten
9. Adolescent
10. Antiseptic
11. Orange
12. Subway
13. Rattlesnake
14. Amiability
15. Sunlight
16. Addiction
17. Harbor
18. Burglar
19. Fructose
20. Chord
21. Desk
22. Shipmate
23. Winnings
24. Earthworm
25. Tinkle
26. Brawn
27. Underworld
28. Pepper
29. Arson
30. Estate
31. Caress
32. Wholesaler
33. Undercurrent

34. Bout
35. Saltine
36. Proxy
37. Misdeed
38. Pliability
39. Kook
40. Recline
41. Olive
42. Crotchet
43. Will
44. Shark
45. Seed
46. Resilience
47. Currant
48. Gulf
49. Heap
50. Snake
51. Italics
52. Hedge
53. Souvenir
54. Census
55. Picture
56. Handbarrow
57. Seafood
58. Unification
59. Headstream
60. Dinner
61. Mentor
62. Backsplash
63. Cane
64. Advantage
65. Imprisonment
66. Headphones
67. Caraway

68. Bramble
69. Inspectorate
70. Houseplant
71. Hangout
72. Ache
73. Filament
74. Opulence
75. Haystack
76. Laborer
77. Charlatan
78. Expletive
79. Animosity
80. Glow
81. Wink
82. Duel
83. Brassiere
84. Fleet
85. Confirmation
86. Presidency
87. Hog
88. Tumbler
89. Smelt
90. Mechanic
91. Panel
92. Genome
93. Convention
94. Peck
95. Overture
96. Radical
97. Overdose
98. Turn
99. Affluence

0. Leer
1. Sunscreen
2. Quota
3. Posy
4. Time
5. Offender
6. Frugality
7. Siren
8. Highlighter
9. Gratitude
10. Majesty
11. Misconduct
12. Perch
13. Spangle
14. Critic
15. Seminar
16. Rebellion
17. Functionary
18. Sequin
19. Nationalist
20. Egotist
21. Waxwork
22. Druggist
23. Phrase
24. Innovation
25. Action
26. Cauliflower
27. Sting
28. Stepladder
29. Rationalism
30. Transfer
31. Crucible
32. Tactics
33. Field
34. Poll
35. Trombone
36. Evacuation
37. Pantry
38. Delicacy
39. Leapfrog
40. Linesman
41. Deficiency
42. Shooter
43. Recession
44. Profession
45. Quarterfinal
46. Cloister
47. Benediction
48. Manhole
49. Nook
50. Mediation
51. Dispenser
52. Hacker
53. Blockade
54. Hinge
55. Merry
56. Igloo
57. Lisp
58. Beneficiary
59. Exaltation
60. Cam
61. Landslip
62. Envy
63. Hiccup
64. Parent
65. Channel
66. Second
67. Yogurt
68. Consul
69. Incapability
70. Angle
71. Deceiver
72. Quince
73. Type
74. Philistine
75. Disposal
76. Materialism
77. Meringue
78. Continuance
79. Frigate
80. Aerobics
81. Protest
82. Director
83. Dungeon
84. Crossroads
85. Nationality
86. Sole
87. Psychiatrist
88. Brimstone
89. Equinox
90. Stride
91. Cake
92. Ghost
93. Knocker
94. Refreshment
95. Yen
96. Initiation
97. Possessor
98. Orchid
99. Array

0. Toddler	34. Binding	68. Student
1. Identification	35. Postscript	69. Extension
2. Telegram	36. Knapsack	70. Motorbike
3. Squirrel	37. Freight	71. Contractor
4. Bronco	38. Epidemic	72. Rest
5. Moisturizer	39. Burb	73. Undercoat
6. Plenty	40. Patronage	74. Vandalism
7. Mustang	41. Elixir	75. Huckleberry
8. Abrasion	42. Troupe	76. Enrollment
9. Brute	43. Carnage	77. Shootout
10. Answer	44. Corrosion	78. Stratosphere
11. Meat	45. Game	79. Phaeton
12. Disrepair	46. Riot	80. Miniature
13. Practitioner	47. Nipple	81. Throttle
14. Cynicism	48. Mustache	82. Beech
15. Delegate	49. Ripple	83. Simplification
16. Chopsticks	50. Truffle	84. Traitor
17. Depth	51. Bodice	85. Admiration
18. Platoon	52. Similarity	86. Hardship
19. Harangue	53. Arrears	87. Gambler
20. Support	54. Gathering	88. Seagull
21. Buccaneer	55. Prompter	89. Rust
22. Maltreatment	56. Chevron	90. Almond
23. Bureaucracy	57. Flogging	91. Mosquito
24. Elation	58. Folklore	92. Neon
25. Merman	59. Affinity	93. Consignment
26. Inconstancy	60. Muck	94. Slight
27. Wax	61. Minesweeper	95. Noise
28. Fellow	62. Sportsman	96. Refraction
29. Browser	63. Crumple	97. Crack
30. Dormitory	64. Shooting	98. Endowment
31. Notability	65. Orbit	99. Record
32. Pheasant	66. Victuals	
33. Realist	67. Junction	

0. Pea
1. Brain
2. Civilization
3. Structure
4. Garden
5. Martyr
6. Aggression
7. Grandmother
8. Sweetheart
9. Ecosystem
10. Snort
11. Turnstile
12. Beetle
13. Roughage
14. Resident
15. Middleweight
16. Midday
17. Accountancy
18. Chemical
19. Femininity
20. Gratuity
21. Floe
22. Eighty
23. Convent
24. Hedgerow
25. Somersault
26. Sultana
27. Sorbet
28. Itinerary
29. Evasion
30. Vessel
31. Duct
32. Censer
33. Sill
34. Quatrain
35. Upshot
36. Melodrama
37. Legislature
38. Leanness
39. Twist
40. Cavalcade
41. Calculation
42. Muse
43. Assassination
44. Songbird
45. Inconvenience
46. Source
47. Lager
48. Software
49. Bidder
50. Pollution
51. Pavilion
52. Joystick
53. Flash
54. Octopus
55. Pleat
56. Syncopation
57. Astonishment
58. Thousand
59. Vapor
60. Supposition
61. Article
62. Newborn
63. Domain
64. Lavender
65. Orienteering
66. Manger
67. Pig
68. Retailer
69. Mist
70. Viper
71. Tooth
72. Snowball
73. Mischief
74. Assemblage
75. Vamp
76. Substitution
77. Fetish
78. Supplement
79. Pirate
80. Component
81. Guffaw
82. Chill
83. Hairdo
84. Kookaburra
85. Forger
86. Vendor
87. Thump
88. Companionway
89. Eyewitness
90. Manufacturer
91. Antacid
92. Diffidence
93. Parade
94. Hide
95. Objector
96. Spread
97. Underwire
98. Ideology
99. Centaur

0. Supermarket	34. Choir	68. Ode
1. Murder	35. Population	69. Room
2. Punch	36. Lorry	70. Kingdom
3. Starling	37. Counsel	71. Nursery
4. Dilution	38. Affiliation	72. Nourishment
5. Nonchalance	39. Brat	73. June
6. Verse	40. Combustion	74. Curriculum
7. Paper	41. Propensity	75. Lemon
8. Pound	42. Breastplate	76. Multiplex
9. Brightness	43. Drudge	77. Essence
10. Freeway	44. Peroration	78. Jubilee
11. Uplift	45. Searcher	79. Wildebeest
12. Preservative	46. Shine	80. Breakwater
13. Kinsman	47. Obscenity	81. Willow
14. Skill	48. Princess	82. Transience
15. Benefactor	49. Resonance	83. Seduction
16. Aspiration	50. Skirt	84. Scull
17. Snag	51. Compliant	85. Banana
18. Scuba	52. Chapel	86. Wisp
19. Birthday	53. Pansy	87. Goatee
20. Nymph	54. Girlfriend	88. Sow
21. Fall	55. Organism	89. Plight
22. Shepherd	56. Derrick	90. Headwaters
23. Onyx	57. Exchange	91. Rampart
24. Chip	58. Slackness	92. Radar
25. Duration	59. Insurance	93. Billet
26. Globalization	60. Customer	94. Antagonism
27. Thunderclap	61. Upgrade	95. Liter
28. Hymn	62. Tendon	96. Mortise
29. Oddment	63. Dogmatism	97. Viceroy
30. Karate	64. Gunsmith	98. Farina
31. Parcel	65. Saboteur	99. Implication
32. Philology	66. Magnolia	
33. Implosion	67. Bond	

0. Incline	34. Prescription	68. Sanitation
1. Sink	35. Czar	69. Disobedience
2. Pardon	36. Eyesore	70. Hijack
3. Mime	37. Difference	71. Governor
4. Goddaughter	38. Turf	72. Force
5. Acetylene	39. Splendor	73. Cricket
6. Timetable	40. Revelry	74. Begonia
7. Mystification	41. Ounce	75. Goal
8. Approach	42. Misgiving	76. Veneer
9. Leisure	43. Airliner	77. Expectancy
10. Collaboration	44. Chick	78. Thirty
11. Spade	45. Massage	79. Shininess
12. Phoenix	46. Rank	80. Menagerie
13. Antidote	47. Rationalist	81. Judiciary
14. Topaz	48. Male	82. Herdsman
15. Ballpoint	49. Painting	83. Smoke
16. Bicycle	50. Verity	84. Folder
17. Lotion	51. Changeling	85. Contributor
18. Bunt	52. Yawn	86. Swagger
19. Engineer	53. Alto	87. Nail
20. Tranquility	54. Wreck	88. Sonata
21. Morbidity	55. Lilac	89. Calypso
22. Collection	56. Ampere	90. Rudeness
23. Dictator	57. Now	91. Coke
24. Strawberry	58. Festivity	92. Worthlessness
25. Foe	59. Seminary	93. Assistance
26. Flute	60. Lathe	94. Skiing
27. Gumption	61. Geology	95. Cavity
28. Gymnast	62. Curator	96. Polestar
29. Ninja	63. Schemer	97. Luncheon
30. Scrubber	64. Soldiery	98. Wanderer
31. Storm	65. Daub	99. Tentacle
32. Plane	66. Plantain	
33. Vengeance	67. Usurer	

0. Methyl
1. Shoelace
2. Phosphate
3. Conservatism
4. Transmutation
5. Farm
6. Gasp
7. Fragrance
8. Cinder
9. Fill
10. Broadcast
11. Stilt
12. Retrospective
13. Doctrine
14. Griddle
15. Hometown
16. Mirage
17. Virago
18. Integrator
19. Funk
20. Marksman
21. Marigold
22. Smith
23. Cutlery
24. Clinic
25. Body
26. Scheme
27. Condolences
28. Serration
29. Satiety
30. Pauper
31. Herbalist
32. Nativity
33. Forty
34. Slang
35. Intensifier
36. Reserve
37. Rant
38. Molehill
39. Millimeter
40. Funnies
41. Wire
42. Drunkenness
43. Illiteracy
44. Duo
45. Torpedo
46. Barge
47. Emperor
48. Honeybee
49. Word
50. Versatility
51. Vitamin
52. Alleviation
53. Footpath
54. Mustard
55. Kitchen
56. Fiesta
57. Finance
58. Orchestra
59. Attic
60. Mismanagement
61. Marmoset
62. Oxen
63. Recipe
64. Vice
65. Impeachment
66. Stonework
67. Jail
68. Plurality
69. Rebuke
70. Taximeter
71. Flair
72. Mosaic
73. Quilt
74. Gyroscope
75. Originality
76. Socket
77. Shabbiness
78. Diminutive
79. Illusion
80. Confession
81. Timidity
82. Genuineness
83. Fuss
84. Nightgown
85. Egotism
86. Elk
87. Sunset
88. Cobweb
89. Oilskin
90. Appreciation
91. Annoyance
92. Treat
93. Theft
94. Screed
95. Search
96. Bloodhound
97. Cuttlefish
98. Perfumery
99. Welder

0. Mind	34. Phial	68. Conciliation
1. Hearth	35. Haziness	69. Streamer
2. Regime	36. Pause	70. Limpet
3. Rain	37. Apartment	71. Dredger
4. Exhibitor	38. Fizz	72. Syringe
5. Nastiness	39. Art	73. Theologian
6. Trepidation	40. Sine	74. Bungalow
7. Preacher	41. Prudence	75. Tether
8. Dilemma	42. Dram	76. Canary
9. Robin	43. Flowerpot	77. Lens
10. Headset	44. Mallet	78. Aspect
11. Object	45. Memory	79. Bridesmaid
12. Perpetuity	46. Solicitation	80. Beauty
13. Sarcasm	47. Bylaw	81. Compilation
14. Wonder	48. Sympathy	82. Parallelogram
15. Ferocity	49. Microwave	83. Welfare
16. Stem	50. Censor	84. Ghoul
17. Irradiation	51. Galaxy	85. Climate
18. Calcium	52. Turnout	86. Keenness
19. Post	53. Flush	87. Understanding
20. Exuberance	54. Ark	88. Dependency
21. Progression	55. Dye	89. Witness
22. Doctorate	56. Corset	90. Fatigue
23. Representation	57. Exile	91. Entanglement
24. Empathy	58. Coronation	92. Administrator
25. Presence	59. Scar	93. Minelayer
26. Prompt	60. Continuity	94. Kerosene
27. Corps	61. Cloakroom	95. Vodka
28. Main	62. Battery	96. Raisin
29. Chant	63. Job	97. Ambulance
30. Lint	64. Relationship	98. Soloist
31. Mayonnaise	65. Vestibule	99. Steeple
32. Foreground	66. Irregularity	
33. Novelist	67. Mark	

0. Aeronautics	34. Recurrence	68. Peephole
1. Lime	35. Thief	69. Gazette
2. Quadrennium	36. Shot	70. Liege
3. Adoration	37. Bookkeeper	71. Jewelry
4. Adage	38. Testimony	72. Sprinkler
5. Diligence	39. Gun	73. Decrease
6. Sighting	40. Lid	74. Blinker
7. History	41. Bolster	75. Beverage
8. Click	42. Spiritualist	76. Perquisite
9. Passivity	43. Mistletoe	77. Status
10. Apostle	44. Narcissism	78. Incisor
11. Drive	45. Trashcan	79. Reader
12. Dignity	46. Spaceship	80. Feud
13. Grind	47. Sod	81. Reflector
14. Generosity	48. Five	82. Thinness
15. Requiem	49. Loop	83. Toilet
16. Handful	50. Sensor	84. Inlet
17. Thread	51. Buzzard	85. Vagrant
18. Wrongdoing	52. Name	86. Enigma
19. Lode	53. Onomatopoeia	87. Axiom
20. Outskirts	54. Pedal	88. Watchman
21. Deftness	55. Exertion	89. Urbanity
22. Sharper	56. Thick	90. Instructor
23. Gate	57. Inside	91. Stink
24. Building	58. Exemption	92. Deviation
25. Anesthesia	59. Media	93. Sheen
26. Past	60. Groove	94. Handbook
27. Distrust	61. Exhibitionist	95. Rashness
28. Ceramics	62. Hardboard	96. Snowplow
29. Moon	63. Journey	97. Succession
30. Mermaid	64. Troop	98. Searchlight
31. Flood	65. Sheriff	99. Stuff
32. Deed	66. Shelf	
33. Chore	67. Simulation	

0. Recount	34. Phenomenon	68. Resort
1. Trooper	35. Sanctuary	69. Jujube
2. Hassle	36. Brake	70. Equator
3. Vehemence	37. Militia	71. Harmony
4. Entail	38. Repose	72. Rogue
5. Ventriloquist	39. Fang	73. Sideburns
6. Tankard	40. Yoga	74. Bushel
7. Peat	41. Nest	75. Secularism
8. Power	42. Tungsten	76. Sainthood
9. Folio	43. Rectangle	77. Silage
10. Salamander	44. Specifics	78. Dejection
11. Platter	45. Spat	79. Reality
12. Onslaught	46. Pacifism	80. Arrow
13. Warrior	47. Cot	81. Livery
14. Caravan	48. Rendezvous	82. Kinship
15. Nationalism	49. Teat	83. Paratrooper
16. Hankie	50. Powder	84. Warbler
17. Upright	51. Pharaoh	85. Calculator
18. Refugee	52. Application	86. Skeleton
19. Can	53. Calm	87. Duplicity
20. Heresy	54. Appetizer	88. Sousaphone
21. Pale	55. Dissension	89. Pebble
22. Glee	56. Fryer	90. Tuba
23. Accordion	57. Retort	91. Wimple
24. Guest	58. Slash	92. Irrigation
25. Strife	59. Huff	93. Supervisor
26. Brigade	60. Iceboat	94. Hold
27. Portrayal	61. Suntan	95. Code
28. Guitar	62. Warden	96. Class
29. Accusation	63. Pitfall	97. Solitaire
30. Fragment	64. Adaptability	98. Owl
31. Nib	65. Reproach	99. Smug
32. Million	66. Maiden	
33. Highness	67. Priest	

0. Quartz	34. Oar	68. Right
1. Wasp	35. Obligee	69. Clipper
2. Fugue	36. Chef	70. Basalt
3. License	37. Rowdiness	71. Inhaler
4. Skit	38. Sleepover	72. Alcoholic
5. Reformer	39. Mollusk	73. Saucer
6. Primrose	40. Turtleneck	74. Snippet
7. Friar	41. Lackey	75. Curd
8. Bit	42. Steakhouse	76. Accord
9. Barbarism	43. Frieze	77. Tow
10. Fix	44. Garnet	78. Destroyer
11. Basis	45. Blight	79. Layman
12. Bellows	46. Nailbrush	80. Rapidity
13. Trauma	47. Hutch	81. Abbey
14. Stationery	48. Luggage	82. Patriot
15. Cable	49. Reminder	83. Metronome
16. Cent	50. Victory	84. Leaning
17. Membrane	51. Elm	85. Famine
18. Athlete	52. Cart	86. Immortality
19. Flint	53. Fledgling	87. Decagon
20. Undercut	54. Vest	88. Indent
21. Wand	55. Summary	89. Noblewoman
22. Leader	56. Transference	90. Termination
23. Extravagance	57. Snorkel	91. Corkscrew
24. Actress	58. Wizard	92. Romper
25. Aperture	59. Audacity	93. Extradition
26. Guesswork	60. Conundrum	94. Episode
27. Archbishop	61. Hayride	95. Family
28. Module	62. Youth	96. Stricture
29. Median	63. Monopoly	97. Inquiry
30. Fairway	64. Pianist	98. Backbone
31. Gimmick	65. Trunks	99. Unbeliever
32. Unhappiness	66. Wavelength	
33. Favoritism	67. Shocker	

0. Gander	34. Vertex	68. Recruit
1. Saturn	35. Artillery	69. Terrorist
2. Extermination	36. Oatmeal	70. Movables
3. Lever	37. Frustration	71. Fodder
4. Couple	38. Usher	72. Nibble
5. Neglect	39. Repression	73. Siphon
6. Leash	40. Exultation	74. Forethought
7. Smut	41. Jeep	75. Conductor
8. Coupling	42. Fanfare	76. Needlework
9. Dealer	43. Pose	77. Salon
10. Notoriety	44. Clump	78. Nanogram
11. Glider	45. Clank	79. Lurch
12. Gibbon	46. Hay	80. Invasion
13. Termite	47. Diplomacy	81. Citizenship
14. Moderation	48. Pub	82. Sundial
15. Blemish	49. Ballast	83. Arrangement
16. Recollection	50. Caper	84. Manners
17. Corral	51. Tube	85. Ordination
18. Credit	52. Avenue	86. Balcony
19. Plaster	53. Rascal	87. Oriole
20. Boatswain	54. Exploit	88. Radioactivity
21. Harmonics	55. Slack	89. Displeasure
22. Perspective	56. Sixty	90. Koala
23. Drought	57. Din	91. Etching
24. Midway	58. Host	92. Seedling
25. Gnome	59. Naughtiness	93. Waders
26. Badge	60. Epitome	94. Fanatic
27. Clan	61. Airport	95. Raspberry
28. Innkeeper	62. Hollow	96. Whisper
29. Intuition	63. Tile	97. Thirteen
30. Sandpaper	64. Poet	98. Management
31. Viscose	65. Watermelon	99. Spy
32. Restraint	66. Horseplay	
33. Outcrop	67. Magnificence	

0. Sunburn	34. Heartwood	68. Llano
1. Polecat	35. Inflation	69. Handspring
2. Concerto	36. Dasher	70. Kit
3. Holocaust	37. Resentment	71. Intermission
4. Charades	38. Strap	72. Edging
5. Charade	39. Stubble	73. Offer
6. Militarism	40. Machinist	74. Egg
7. Footing	41. Kerchief	75. Chance
8. Archipelago	42. Plague	76. Peppercorn
9. Contender	43. Woe	77. Immunity
10. Stick	44. Abuse	78. Hula
11. Scrutiny	45. Midwifery	79. Sweat
12. Remand	46. Oxide	80. Anagram
13. Limit	47. Jive	81. Tapioca
14. Cog	48. Hoodlum	82. Mandolin
15. Groan	49. Assessment	83. Parody
16. Forum	50. Scuttle	84. Insinuation
17. Cab	51. Gorge	85. Sidewinder
18. Intoxication	52. Poem	86. Crammer
19. Hire	53. Vestige	87. Tug
20. Tomato	54. Countess	88. Temerity
21. Exit	55. Chameleon	89. Origami
22. Spontaneity	56. Complexity	90. Stencil
23. Gosling	57. Characteristic	91. Midwife
24. Bayonet	58. Sphinx	92. Expiry
25. Fame	59. Weasel	93. Guise
26. Laboratory	60. Pipe	94. Consternation
27. Judge	61. Cereal	95. Plausibility
28. Politics	62. Clutch	96. Animal
29. Territory	63. Disintegration	97. World
30. Gaggle	64. Transportation	98. Stockholder
31. Drag	65. Pine	99. Cheese
32. Marsh	66. Share	
33. Ling	67. Mountaineer	

0. Paperweight
1. Hare
2. Morals
3. Demonstrator
4. Impossibility
5. Responsibility
6. Bouquet
7. Enticement
8. Silicon
9. Communist
10. Triumph
11. Tormentor
12. Sparkler
13. Thong
14. Aurora
15. Amp
16. Chink
17. Pharmacy
18. Bulldozer
19. Dispensation
20. Locker
21. Utility
22. Palisades
23. Gloom
24. Fin
25. Sovereignty
26. Professor
27. Miscalculation
28. Wares
29. Brethren
30. Buffoon
31. Bluff
32. Burglary
33. Species
34. Mash
35. Tiara
36. Memento
37. Cockroach
38. Condemnation
39. Validity
40. Confidant
41. Detriment
42. Muzzle
43. Oration
44. Credence
45. Intemperance
46. Snowflake
47. Haircut
48. Leg
49. Quartering
50. Inconsistency
51. Wrestler
52. Humanism
53. Appetite
54. Incredibility
55. Tachometer
56. Supporter
57. Personality
58. Sanctions
59. Don
60. Nickname
61. Cymbal
62. Chasm
63. Rugby
64. Idiot
65. Apartheid
66. Stabling
67. Semblance
68. Negligee
69. Sovereign
70. Admittance
71. Firstborn
72. Rating
73. Protrusion
74. Lawyer
75. Bankrupt
76. Rink
77. Alphabet
78. Flatware
79. Indignity
80. Laceration
81. Retardation
82. Brownie
83. Rental
84. Debut
85. Reckoning
86. Barn
87. Fort
88. Peony
89. Canon
90. Chauffeur
91. Talent
92. Fur
93. Upkeep
94. Opportunist
95. Lodestone
96. Divinity
97. Occurrence
98. Disclosure
99. Phonics

0. Predecessor
1. Silk
2. Journeyman
3. Repulse
4. Soybean
5. Gale
6. Appearance
7. Pleasure
8. Profusion
9. Visit
10. Newsletter
11. Monocle
12. Service
13. Outpost
14. Castle
15. Surcharge
16. Fastening
17. Barb
18. Vassal
19. Impudence
20. Mud
21. Lion
22. Capitalist
23. Tarantula
24. Hex
25. Flop
26. Hike
27. Porter
28. Concertina
29. Jug
30. Proprietor
31. Skid
32. Fridge
33. Spritzer
34. Scientist
35. Reinforcement
36. Descendant
37. Torture
38. Reliance
39. Carpenter
40. Cabinet
41. Hectare
42. Scrag
43. Commentator
44. Mitt
45. Asthma
46. Psalm
47. Kibbutznik
48. Parity
49. Yeoman
50. Sunstroke
51. Bill
52. Saturation
53. Patty
54. Decibel
55. Triplet
56. Nocturne
57. Curtness
58. Outlook
59. Merchandise
60. Ore
61. Boutique
62. Giant
63. Alp
64. Aster
65. Squire
66. Swimsuit
67. Degree
68. Prude
69. Radium
70. Overthrow
71. Kilometer
72. Dissembler
73. Distribution
74. Darkness
75. Partiality
76. Hitch
77. Clamber
78. Puddle
79. Decree
80. Amphitheater
81. Morale
82. Gap
83. Nervousness
84. Bark
85. Treadle
86. Pumpkin
87. Hart
88. Insomnia
89. Hydrant
90. Gas
91. Graphics
92. Pedestal
93. Morality
94. Wash
95. Resolve
96. Gargoyle
97. Raffle
98. Formation
99. Proscription

0. Spectrum
1. Railroad
2. Seltzer
3. Walkover
4. April
5. Wile
6. Selector
7. Tribe
8. Husk
9. Rainfall
10. Refill
11. Observatory
12. Spacing
13. Sparrow
14. Mistrust
15. Flapjack
16. Auk
17. Blindness
18. Livelihood
19. Logic
20. Routine
21. Schooling
22. Dagger
23. Babe
24. Alternative
25. Segmentation
26. Porch
27. Preface
28. Thermometer
29. Scrimmage
30. Mohair
31. Cycle
32. Subordination
33. Formality
34. Scorn
35. Siding
36. Mutant
37. Horror
38. Tights
39. Matriculation
40. Proposition
41. Video
42. Glare
43. Fifth
44. Solder
45. Dowry
46. Lumberjack
47. Oarlock
48. Paradox
49. Unicorn
50. Sneeze
51. Metamorphosis
52. Beret
53. Compatriot
54. Triangle
55. Lout
56. Whim
57. Escape
58. Teal
59. Ether
60. Gibe
61. Hamper
62. Ruff
63. Revenge
64. Position
65. Gypsy
66. Pew
67. Intervention
68. Merchant
69. Tiger
70. Watercress
71. Confusion
72. Interval
73. Signature
74. Bewilderment
75. Rendering
76. Ovation
77. Visa
78. Maker
79. Inertia
80. Writings
81. Lunatic
82. Reassurance
83. Crowd
84. Trash
85. Favor
86. Running
87. Treason
88. Leek
89. Eggplant
90. Board
91. Luxury
92. Whist
93. Regimentation
94. Piety
95. Tabulation
96. Mattress
97. Park
98. Scale
99. Void

0. Rosewood	34. Radiation	68. Butt
1. Crookedness	35. Graphite	69. Rumble
2. Umpire	36. Coffee	70. Grid
3. Conquest	37. Alloy	71. Fray
4. Piece	38. Reprint	72. Microscope
5. Nerve	39. Heptagon	73. Nil
6. Stripe	40. Pungency	74. Mantilla
7. Clinch	41. Hemp	75. Bonbon
8. Decimal	42. Scavenger	76. Convert
9. Diagram	43. Sloth	77. Splashdown
10. Spasm	44. Gamble	78. Innocence
11. Pinch	45. Manslaughter	79. Pertness
12. Graphic	46. Hypothermia	80. Ditto
13. Lewdness	47. Seaplane	81. Bedspread
14. Nobility	48. Soil	82. Idleness
15. Drove	49. Password	83. Prick
16. Turban	50. Anteater	84. Twig
17. Valuables	51. Temperate	85. Monitor
18. Nebula	52. Dateline	86. Cage
19. Line	53. Drifter	87. Sonnet
20. Tuft	54. Kapok	88. Telegraphy
21. Productivity	55. Prize	89. Meow
22. Conservation	56. Fulmar	90. Sanctimony
23. Blend	57. Jeans	91. Target
24. Transport	58. Helmet	92. Tabby
25. Seduce	59. Dolphin	93. Stalk
26. Abnormality	60. Gala	94. Triviality
27. Four	61. Tabernacle	95. Hickory
28. Falseness	62. Crane	96. Demon
29. Constrictor	63. Fez	97. Journal
30. Tag	64. Deck	98. Emblem
31. Horseshoe	65. Pistil	99. Yearning
32. Equity	66. Subpoena	
33. Case	67. Stowaway	

0. Groom	34. Trusteeship	68. Doughnut
1. Original	35. Ostracism	69. Transformation
2. Ricochet	36. Barber	70. Stamina
3. Feint	37. Synopsis	71. Pat
4. Score	38. Explosion	72. Fax
5. Muffin	39. Apostrophe	73. Ramification
6. Expiration	40. Knee	74. Delinquent
7. Mistake	41. Fan	75. Paring
8. Jest	42. Mine	76. Timekeeper
9. Senior	43. Concourse	77. Cobbler
10. Sapling	44. Mower	78. Altruism
11. Nachos	45. Boycott	79. Ravioli
12. Wretch	46. Permutation	80. Hatchway
13. Reply	47. Agenda	81. Shortbread
14. Ass	48. Request	82. Hamster
15. Licensee	49. Shareware	83. Hearing
16. Indicator	50. Meal	84. Trampoline
17. Understatement	51. Skylight	85. Exponent
18. Walnut	52. Warrant	86. Settlement
19. Liberal	53. Temper	87. Probability
20. Division	54. Stylist	88. Trio
21. Amenities	55. Moneylender	89. String
22. Premonition	56. Vindication	90. Bosom
23. Aborigine	57. Inkblot	91. Public
24. Gridiron	58. Placard	92. Headstand
25. Fraction	59. Pun	93. Quagmire
26. Memo	60. Anecdote	94. Pronouncement
27. Loom	61. Capitalism	95. Ferret
28. Serge	62. Sax	96. Reinstatement
29. Porcelain	63. Tinsel	97. Syntax
30. Glucose	64. Automation	98. Postage
31. Suppression	65. Retrospect	99. Sob
32. Redhead	66. Freighter	
33. Liquor	67. Form	

0. Antler	34. Obscurity	68. Hallucination
1. Company	35. Vulnerability	69. Armadillo
2. Extract	36. Ravages	70. Heading
3. Hazard	37. Windward	71. Vixen
4. Typesetter	38. Edit	72. Dame
5. Vexation	39. Planet	73. Dissident
6. Import	40. Principle	74. Project
7. Bandit	41. Glimpse	75. Seclusion
8. Visionary	42. Church	76. Hybrid
9. Hank	43. Pendulum	77. Education
10. Congenial	44. Untouchable	78. Surprise
11. Horizon	45. Adolescence	79. Scope
12. Cataract	46. Opportunity	80. Tumult
13. Landlady	47. Ottoman	81. Mix
14. Heft	48. Executor	82. Conscience
15. Truth	49. Lull	83. Magenta
16. Framer	50. Fiberglass	84. Guardian
17. Corridor	51. Latrine	85. Liberality
18. Row	52. Truce	86. Flower
19. Kiss	53. Document	87. Armor
20. Film	54. Upholstery	88. Jet
21. Flora	55. Dare	89. Wheelbarrow
22. Satori	56. Eagle	90. Wick
23. Chorus	57. Compromise	91. Hole
24. Schoolteacher	58. Ski	92. Familiar
25. Retention	59. Treasurer	93. Viewer
26. Snub	60. Thug	94. Preservation
27. Compass	61. Pollen	95. Plaice
28. Receptive	62. Weekend	96. Ruffian
29. Dive	63. May	97. Knack
30. Demand	64. Chairman	98. Mare
31. Parapet	65. Advocate	99. Truncheon
32. Hymnal	66. Omission	
33. Parole	67. Junkyard	

0. Switch
1. Mushroom
2. Allotment
3. Surrogate
4. Pucker
5. Surrender
6. Daring
7. Display
8. Gunshot
9. Archer
10. Gist
11. Hop
12. Magician
13. Transition
14. Heaviness
15. Phobia
16. Ferment
17. Rent
18. Kinetics
19. Chlorophyll
20. Drapes
21. Photography
22. Stroller
23. Suppressant
24. Cruelty
25. Locality
26. Turnpike
27. Guild
28. Hoist
29. Compliment
30. Enamel
31. Caption
32. Ancestry
33. Behavior
34. Drubbing
35. Cocoa
36. Twang
37. Relic
38. Tapestry
39. Folly
40. Taper
41. Dullard
42. Buttercup
43. Bedroom
44. Flavoring
45. Dudgeon
46. Humiliation
47. Elimination
48. Scenery
49. Shoulder
50. Amount
51. Whir
52. Relay
53. Coupon
54. Savagery
55. Cactus
56. Marshal
57. Centimeter
58. Download
59. Wrap
60. Glitter
61. Verbosity
62. Falconry
63. Revulsion
64. Inroad
65. Performance
66. Teeth
67. Enhancement
68. Fluff
69. Abyss
70. Flourish
71. Petunia
72. Guy
73. Irrationalism
74. Bully
75. Carbon
76. Mooring
77. Hibernation
78. Sulfur
79. Congruity
80. Grumbler
81. Musquash
82. Cupful
83. Tidbit
84. Kindred
85. Cuckoo
86. Justification
87. Aardvark
88. Displacement
89. Guard
90. Van
91. Ridder
92. Hyphen
93. Slipknot
94. Dab
95. Parable
96. Hornist
97. Transit
98. Promenade
99. Cookery

0. Realm
1. Transmitter
2. Pang
3. Judicial
4. Climax
5. Abalone
6. Anger
7. Clam
8. Starvation
9. Multitude
10. Alliance
11. Prosperity
12. Splint
13. Teamwork
14. Headrest
15. Recrimination
16. Steppe
17. Paddle
18. Quad
19. Completion
20. Insole
21. Heritage
22. Procedure
23. Tyranny
24. Feat
25. Delegation
26. Quiche
27. Treachery
28. Conger
29. Columbine
30. Disgrace
31. Icicle
32. Thaw
33. Slave
34. Colander
35. Valuation
36. Felt
37. Politeness
38. Gymnasium
39. Speller
40. Prerogative
41. Frivolity
42. Occasion
43. Handler
44. Stallion
45. Minister
46. Advent
47. Emancipation
48. Belle
49. Jaunt
50. Savior
51. Coalition
52. Handball
53. Facet
54. Standing
55. Turbot
56. Ingredient
57. Clutter
58. Loon
59. Studio
60. Consent
61. Pomp
62. Outcome
63. Illegitimacy
64. Attribute
65. Inspection
66. Back
67. Soldier
68. Compliance
69. Villain
70. Temperament
71. Sundae
72. Limestone
73. Indelicacy
74. Breadwinner
75. Opus
76. Sextuplet
77. Electron
78. Miner
79. Roadhouse
80. Watchword
81. Mount
82. Disparity
83. Staircase
84. Nine
85. Hyperbole
86. Blessing
87. Objective
88. Gangster
89. Palm
90. Jetty
91. Willpower
92. Caprice
93. Father
94. Senator
95. Fielder
96. Nub
97. Bulldog
98. Pact
99. Stanza

0. Archeology	34. Salina	68. Artistry
1. Outgoings	35. Eleven	69. Headsail
2. Baroness	36. Pier	70. Offspring
3. Blubber	37. Royalist	71. Tree
4. Vermin	38. Embankment	72. Marriage
5. Apprentice	39. Imbalance	73. Foothills
6. Anarchy	40. Abundance	74. Staff
7. Shallot	41. Poke	75. Drumstick
8. Romance	42. Inmate	76. Trespasser
9. Brow	43. Chamber	77. Trimester
10. Surrogacy	44. Likes	78. Profiteer
11. Remorse	45. Reimbursement	79. Sculptor
12. Dachshund	46. Faun	80. Fabrication
13. Mentality	47. Reticence	81. Shoot
14. Demonstration	48. Isle	82. Sheepskin
15. Myth	49. Toucan	83. Lighthouse
16. Mainframe	50. Relevance	84. Day
17. Upheaval	51. Burlesque	85. Sermon
18. Whimper	52. Mill	86. Mediator
19. Toadstool	53. Subscriber	87. Wayside
20. Petulance	54. Cantaloupe	88. Horseshoes
21. Lightship	55. Flooring	89. Inadvertence
22. Dirt	56. Semicolon	90. Creator
23. Amphibian	57. Drug	91. Defense
24. Control	58. Rhinoceros	92. Visitation
25. Rope	59. Indecency	93. Rejuvenation
26. Deployment	60. Eight	94. Cloudburst
27. Impact	61. Mound	95. Ad
28. Rum	62. Angel	96. Thrift
29. Latch	63. Hint	97. Flume
30. Curry	64. Overhead	98. Twelfth
31. Adventure	65. Suit	99. Star
32. Soundtrack	66. Wish	
33. Newness	67. Twine	

0. Orb
1. Orthodoxy
2. Information
3. Rancher
4. Lagoon
5. Vista
6. Paranoia
7. Abduction
8. Tailor
9. Coercion
10. Eminence
11. Sketchbook
12. Skin
13. Footstep
14. Axis
15. Testatrix
16. Shoehorn
17. People
18. Llama
19. Disarray
20. Obstruction
21. Chunk
22. Procession
23. Forecast
24. Marine
25. Sufficiency
26. Bitterness
27. Sun
28. Monkey
29. Springboard
30. Abbot
31. Fluctuation
32. Genesis
33. Consolidation
34. Midshipman
35. Cutlet
36. Stern
37. Radius
38. Softener
39. Mink
40. Approximation
41. Comment
42. Independence
43. Wafer
44. Virgin
45. Militarist
46. Apparatus
47. Member
48. Check
49. Training
50. Blueprint
51. Suite
52. Generation
53. Devastation
54. Distance
55. Dominion
56. Crunch
57. Tunic
58. Enunciation
59. Constituency
60. Strainer
61. Dell
62. Publication
63. Scrubs
64. Distillery
65. Determination
66. Crevasse
67. Cayenne
68. Plinth
69. Cucumber
70. Comparison
71. Destruction
72. Rubbish
73. Persecution
74. Prodigy
75. Confessional
76. Boxing
77. Arm
78. Examination
79. Pastime
80. Trespass
81. Commercial
82. Composition
83. Footlights
84. Projector
85. Appeasement
86. Image
87. Celebrity
88. Raft
89. Sauce
90. Replenishment
91. Diary
92. Civics
93. Constraint
94. Sprout
95. Whisk
96. Penitentiary
97. Vegetarian
98. Employer
99. Peep

0. Refuge	34. Abode	68. Yield
1. Politician	35. Blame	69. Pedicure
2. Nightjar	36. Empire	70. Suspension
3. Swarm	37. Hourglass	71. Tailcoat
4. Chiffon	38. Imitation	72. Dodo
5. Cattle	39. Secession	73. Insufficiency
6. Sailplane	40. Potency	74. Coil
7. Guerrilla	41. Sponge	75. Testament
8. Sediment	42. Confessor	76. Surveillance
9. Lasso	43. Monotone	77. Phase
10. Unbelief	44. Sanitarium	78. Sphere
11. Conquer	45. Grief	79. Revolt
12. Indifference	46. Prawn	80. Spark
13. Sprinkles	47. Crawl	81. Proofreader
14. Fluid	48. Preference	82. Objection
15. Pain	49. Disloyalty	83. Prohibition
16. Cyclist	50. Glasses	84. Tributary
17. Lifebuoy	51. December	85. Axle
18. Junior	52. Sniff	86. Nimbus
19. Tetrahedron	53. Exhalation	87. Oak
20. Community	54. Tackiness	88. Eye
21. Pickle	55. Booth	89. Drawer
22. Lichen	56. Business	90. Delivery
23. Knowledge	57. Factor	91. Moorcock
24. Blackout	58. Worry	92. Quarantine
25. Prudery	59. Stoicism	93. Caramel
26. Beam	60. Toxicologist	94. Pneumatics
27. Predominance	61. Correspondence	95. Corollary
28. Conglomeration	62. Veterinarian	96. Fat
29. Orphan	63. Tale	97. Prodigal
30. Grave	64. Blue	98. Intolerance
31. Inquisition	65. Desolation	99. Reprisal
32. Mass	66. Habitat	
33. Turtle	67. Sauerkraut	

0. Item	34. Blockhead	68. Grumble
1. Attendant	35. Stance	69. Cranny
2. Infancy	36. Dialect	70. Level
3. Fever	37. Sleigh	71. Numeral
4. Six	38. Quotation	72. Psychopath
5. Stereo	39. Sister	73. Cluster
6. Dimension	40. Cashmere	74. Sausage
7. Nestling	41. Patsy	75. Oppression
8. Tier	42. Butler	76. Expression
9. Vent	43. Hospitality	77. Crowbar
10. Shield	44. Multiplier	78. Herbivore
11. Dessert	45. Magnum	79. Penitence
12. Thud	46. Snapshot	80. Harmonium
13. Withdrawal	47. Freshman	81. Vulgarity
14. Heat	48. Steam	82. Research
15. Illustration	49. Advisability	83. Stir
16. Kindergarten	50. Ill	84. Chicory
17. Impatience	51. Retribution	85. Remainder
18. Hatred	52. Reiteration	86. Slump
19. Dubiety	53. Stapler	87. Existence
20. Pirouette	54. Minutiae	88. Whinny
21. Solitude	55. Beet	89. Peril
22. Precipitation	56. Profit	90. Box
23. Paisa	57. Hill	91. Piper
24. Friendship	58. Bend	92. Sewer
25. Granny	59. Mean	93. Webbing
26. Valve	60. Emigration	94. Opal
27. Racetrack	61. Greatness	95. Trek
28. Receiver	62. Astuteness	96. Ranch
29. Apprehension	63. Paragraph	97. Trellis
30. Enclosure	64. Cove	98. Clover
31. Result	65. Cacao	99. Hardiness
32. Ketchup	66. Defeatism	
33. Sandalwood	67. Roulette	

0. Furnace	34. Militancy	68. Screwdriver
1. Lampoon	35. Policeman	69. Playwright
2. Spouse	36. Linguistics	70. Jotter
3. Podcast	37. Venture	71. Deceit
4. Bust	38. Lubricant	72. War
5. Encore	39. Sago	73. Dodger
6. Exercise	40. Comfort	74. Football
7. Gunner	41. Tender	75. Whimsy
8. Meddler	42. Vicarage	76. Eviction
9. Sheikh	43. Organist	77. Rhapsody
10. Variation	44. Godliness	78. Enterprise
11. Kibbutz	45. Vilification	79. Quadruplet
12. Spar	46. Jeweler	80. Flight
13. Integration	47. Shoe	81. Shell
14. Drizzle	48. Byway	82. Grove
15. Foot	49. Cut	83. Breeze
16. Canter	50. Insularity	84. Shorts
17. Dilapidation	51. Candor	85. Yogi
18. Conscript	52. Song	86. Headliner
19. Feel	53. Window	87. Oboe
20. Compression	54. Lightning	88. Fiend
21. Dotage	55. Inhabitant	89. Commodity
22. Predisposition	56. Shirker	90. Rehearsal
23. Maturity	57. Complicity	91. Light
24. Mars	58. Stretcher	92. Ranter
25. Incense	59. Soup	93. Mister
26. Checkmate	60. Sensation	94. Auto
27. Scream	61. Character	95. Quibble
28. Lasagna	62. Panache	96. Shortcoming
29. Lifeboat	63. Scoreboard	97. Kebab
30. Aroma	64. Conservatory	98. Emulsion
31. Goldsmith	65. Contingency	99. Spore
32. Smelter	66. Pastor	
33. Aide	67. Joke	

0. Holograph
1. Vitals
2. Arbitration
3. Precipice
4. Mommy
5. Consistency
6. Handiwork
7. Sandiness
8. Fantasy
9. Totalitarian
10. Discontent
11. Tarpaulin
12. Merit
13. Scaffolding
14. Registrar
15. Birthright
16. Permit
17. Circus
18. Namesake
19. Petrology
20. Prowess
21. Camphor
22. Suspenders
23. Straits
24. Ordeal
25. Pulsation
26. Schooner
27. Waterspout
28. Barnacle
29. Rift
30. Whale
31. Tedium
32. Backer
33. Forfeit
34. Heptathlon
35. Congregation
36. Forefront
37. Radiography
38. Shyness
39. Pearl
40. Courier
41. Subtitle
42. Gladness
43. Affair
44. Chastity
45. Dispersion
46. Lamb
47. Change
48. Songbook
49. Convection
50. Transmission
51. Ligature
52. Cashier
53. Forgiveness
54. Vagary
55. Scoundrel
56. Paramedic
57. Ceiling
58. Fiber
59. Nuptials
60. Hilarity
61. Apricot
62. Maple
63. Seedbed
64. Coo
65. Claw
66. Fir
67. Website
68. Precocity
69. Aspen
70. Gibberish
71. Dealings
72. Tremor
73. Heroics
74. Apron
75. Tattletale
76. Tear
77. Dominance
78. Definition
79. Alteration
80. Gender
81. Tracery
82. Surf
83. Ribaldry
84. Hoax
85. Flu
86. Convict
87. Shade
88. Rarity
89. Land
90. Contestant
91. Still
92. Heiress
93. Schism
94. Mango
95. Lord
96. Dent
97. Snack
98. Leviathan
99. Razor

0. Sign
1. Relish
2. Dreadlocks
3. Comet
4. Architect
5. Conjugation
6. Segment
7. Poppy
8. Issue
9. Obesity
10. Gondola
11. Elector
12. Kiln
13. Negotiation
14. Semaphore
15. Ballet
16. Mixture
17. Greeting
18. Embarrassment
19. Onion
20. Slab
21. Closure
22. Witch
23. Price
24. Intruder
25. Volatility
26. Zealot
27. Shortening
28. Skyline
29. Newsreel
30. Legacy
31. Slob
32. Flowchart
33. Sheepdog
34. Frogman
35. Superior
36. Boarder
37. Putt
38. Conformity
39. Recommendation
40. Narcissus
41. Preserve
42. Tribunal
43. Dummy
44. Thieves
45. Wattle
46. Rag
47. Tracing
48. Uprising
49. Highway
50. Integral
51. Flex
52. Rayon
53. Shambles
54. Balderdash
55. Erection
56. Snare
57. Broccoli
58. Remnant
59. Carpet
60. Seaport
61. Gourmet
62. Tape
63. Fallow
64. Burial
65. Fancy
66. Computer
67. Sorcerer
68. Plasma
69. Certainty
70. Satisfaction
71. Mandarin
72. Manuscript
73. Showroom
74. Wayfarer
75. Grounds
76. Grunt
77. Fishhook
78. Program
79. Breath
80. Question
81. Statistician
82. Shortstop
83. Imposter
84. Immersion
85. Writer
86. Fast
87. Brigand
88. Honk
89. Wheat
90. Stay
91. Jam
92. Inspector
93. Layer
94. Seal
95. Grudge
96. Extra
97. Rite
98. Pertinence
99. Masseur

0. Due	34. Galoshes	68. Polish
1. Flake	35. Prosecution	69. Copperplate
2. Fundamentals	36. Whit	70. Delirium
3. Immaturity	37. Manure	71. Blackboard
4. Papaya	38. Quail	72. Odometer
5. Delusion	39. Page	73. Actor
6. Scratch	40. Lobster	74. Transparency
7. Meadow	41. Treasure	75. Cracker
8. Spider	42. Tuck	76. Convexity
9. Pigment	43. Fear	77. Outrider
10. Pulse	44. Duplicate	78. Larch
11. Photocopy	45. Fruition	79. Coffin
12. Highlight	46. Testator	80. Glycerin
13. Option	47. Musk	81. Talk
14. Extenuation	48. Rip	82. Sand
15. Fence	49. Bard	83. Genius
16. Hammer	50. Paparazzi	84. Bole
17. Villager	51. July	85. Chisel
18. Concordance	52. Footprint	86. Spirit
19. Admission	53. Incubation	87. Drill
20. Litany	54. Venus	88. Reindeer
21. Roll	55. Perseverance	89. Nickelodeon
22. Hose	56. Trail	90. Slam
23. Cellophane	57. Cramp	91. Radish
24. Intensity	58. Insulator	92. Ant
25. Bleakness	59. Concert	93. Hostage
26. Reporter	60. Degradation	94. Azure
27. Depression	61. Mascot	95. Duffel
28. Area	62. Taxicab	96. Scythe
29. Tattoo	63. Outcry	97. Mallard
30. Computation	64. Cowboy	98. Pathologist
31. Stunner	65. Passion	99. Penny
32. Ring	66. Carnival	
33. Difficulty	67. Hydrogen	

0. Attachment
1. Magpie
2. Goalkeeper
3. Seaweed
4. Underground
5. Poster
6. Collector
7. Banquet
8. Stalemate
9. Quiz
10. Reef
11. Acclamation
12. Title
13. Contiguity
14. Fleece
15. Champagne
16. Fork
17. Fun
18. Womenfolk
19. Joust
20. Motion
21. March
22. Pelt
23. Pike
24. Scholarship
25. Gelignite
26. Heron
27. Elegy
28. Locomotion
29. Wisdom
30. Stopper
31. Navy
32. Coherence
33. Knave
34. Arbitrator
35. Millionaire
36. Bottle
37. Mask
38. Expansion
39. Ornamentation
40. Handbill
41. Repetition
42. Sangria
43. Debt
44. Counterfeiter
45. Pluralist
46. Revolution
47. Home
48. Rose
49. Ride
50. Questionnaire
51. Sandbox
52. Duckling
53. Macaroon
54. Spaetzle
55. Platform
56. Rickshaw
57. Trapezium
58. Edge
59. Promoter
60. Settler
61. Sandal
62. Mildness
63. Rockery
64. Hoot
65. Distinction
66. Motorway
67. Harvest
68. Master
69. Upbeat
70. Amusement
71. Obligation
72. Domination
73. Pronunciation
74. Fountain
75. Purpose
76. Deer
77. Plastic
78. Presumption
79. Brown
80. Toaster
81. Proton
82. Grounding
83. Enrichment
84. Mantel
85. Novelty
86. Learning
87. Barricade
88. Bough
89. Counselor
90. Nation
91. Susceptibility
92. Forest
93. Compensation
94. Heavyweight
95. Balk
96. Conciseness
97. Piccolo
98. Apprenticeship
99. Cornice

0. Buttonhole
1. Jersey
2. Pursuit
3. Suffragette
4. Universe
5. Hydrology
6. Nutmeg
7. Sealskin
8. Icon
9. Brushwood
10. Contemplation
11. Advertisement
12. Paleontology
13. Intimacy
14. Conduct
15. Hatchling
16. Boor
17. Puncture
18. Airmail
19. Kiwi
20. Hesitance
21. Rescue
22. Clearing
23. Martyrdom
24. Bass
25. Swimmer
26. Notion
27. Pillar
28. Space
29. Twinkling
30. Stingray
31. Legionary
32. Scrape
33. Perjury
34. Peach
35. Amelioration
36. Blush
37. Monarchy
38. Neptune
39. Provision
40. Herb
41. Tablespoon
42. Gruel
43. Monogram
44. Slider
45. Broomstick
46. Courage
47. Fingertips
48. Lawsuit
49. Hypothesis
50. Solution
51. Jojoba
52. Hurt
53. Newsstand
54. Ripeness
55. Failure
56. Coot
57. Semester
58. Sashimi
59. Paternity
60. Kangaroo
61. Chaperone
62. Dinghy
63. Underclothing
64. Bog
65. Denunciation
66. Kedgeree
67. Salami
68. Cup
69. Intake
70. Grinder
71. Bran
72. Seventh
73. Holly
74. Vehicle
75. Hummingbird
76. Petticoat
77. Outlaw
78. Pixel
79. Violence
80. Sprig
81. Scrub
82. Estimation
83. Money
84. Mainland
85. Comedian
86. Turmoil
87. Like
88. Copy
89. Acknowledgment
90. Starfish
91. Departure
92. Shake
93. Effigy
94. Removal
95. Turnover
96. Psychoanalysis
97. Levy
98. Top
99. Squad

0. Ramp	34. Forefather	68. Rung
1. Swastika	35. Seismograph	69. Washbowl
2. Ministry	36. Calling	70. Slander
3. Forester	37. Ecstasy	71. Tongue
4. Visor	38. Decanter	72. Fig
5. Helm	39. Guile	73. Mangrove
6. Conversation	40. Surface	74. Baguette
7. Lava	41. Boundary	75. Sodium
8. Misfire	42. Newcomer	76. Drainage
9. Twentieth	43. Repeat	77. Syllable
10. Sir	44. Moorage	78. Sociologist
11. Investigator	45. Atom	79. Gambling
12. Fatherhood	46. Warp	80. Ramble
13. Tidiness	47. Humidity	81. Kink
14. Tract	48. Petitioner	82. Charge
15. Carousel	49. Swamp	83. Turnip
16. Blackbird	50. Philanderer	84. Statute
17. Chutney	51. Macaroni	85. Bridle
18. Predestination	52. Buzz	86. Arrowroot
19. Licking	53. Win	87. Daylight
20. Black	54. Agent	88. Eclipse
21. Affectation	55. Rodeo	89. Cubicle
22. Quadratic	56. Scowl	90. Elasticity
23. Twinge	57. Employment	91. Typewriter
24. Capsule	58. Revenue	92. Sash
25. Vacation	59. Scam	93. Ale
26. Guillotine	60. Palette	94. Strudel
27. Hayloft	61. Boll	95. Millennium
28. Muddle	62. Specification	96. Tan
29. Devise	63. Sobriety	97. Seventeen
30. Precedence	64. Bonfire	98. Croak
31. Appointment	65. Repellent	99. Kingfisher
32. Windmill	66. Moorland	
33. Infrequency	67. Agnostic	

0. Statesman
1. Cherub
2. Syrup
3. Entry
4. Excerpt
5. Coming
6. Indication
7. Brooch
8. Upside
9. Acorn
10. Verdigris
11. Addition
12. Blast
13. Continuation
14. Timber
15. Hook
16. Cameo
17. Attendance
18. Carbohydrate
19. Flutter
20. Spitfire
21. Syndicate
22. Jacket
23. Manganese
24. Helicopter
25. Whack
26. Earnings
27. Punster
28. Racist
29. Philanthropist
30. Suitor
31. Favorite
32. Clarification
33. Scan
34. Principality
35. Separation
36. Cantor
37. Freethinker
38. Pedant
39. Jerkin
40. Blueberry
41. Aluminum
42. Sulfate
43. Headway
44. Capital
45. Chicanery
46. Wonderment
47. Bigot
48. Panties
49. Royalty
50. Context
51. Yeast
52. Unrest
53. Complexion
54. Stunt
55. Alcove
56. Ruck
57. Logician
58. Airing
59. Crux
60. Scatterbrain
61. Flounder
62. Daddy
63. Dermatology
64. Resignation
65. Transfusion
66. Sprint
67. Incantation
68. Dynamite
69. Verve
70. Envelope
71. Humanity
72. Harpsichord
73. Cupboard
74. Biology
75. Elopement
76. Julep
77. Ruling
78. Swash
79. Collar
80. Ball
81. Halo
82. Brink
83. Flatness
84. Crater
85. Assurance
86. Tigress
87. Seaside
88. Bedstead
89. Toy
90. Predicate
91. Goodbye
92. Serf
93. Daughter
94. Shortcut
95. Assimilation
96. Injury
97. Hairpiece
98. Hit
99. Arc

0. Linchpin
1. Elder
2. Keg
3. Landscape
4. Alfalfa
5. Depository
6. Guidance
7. Prospector
8. Bailiff
9. Lottery
10. Matrimony
11. Vitriol
12. Viciousness
13. Dear
14. Sixteenth
15. Newsprint
16. Synonym
17. Midst
18. Council
19. Lubrication
20. Lowland
21. Infinity
22. Perforation
23. Imam
24. Arras
25. Electrician
26. Seraph
27. Misery
28. Pancake
29. Sampler
30. Scallywag
31. Exposure
32. Impotence
33. Burr
34. Erosion
35. Experience
36. Compassion
37. Grass
38. Error
39. Pattern
40. Skylark
41. Invoice
42. Regatta
43. Perception
44. Nosepiece
45. Allegation
46. Confluence
47. Dike
48. Ballad
49. Astronaut
50. Stroganoff
51. Vintage
52. Goodness
53. Headquarters
54. Aristocracy
55. Bunny
56. Dissipation
57. Measurement
58. Enlightenment
59. Propagandist
60. Tribulation
61. Diploma
62. Quip
63. Masonry
64. Detraction
65. Workforce
66. Solarium
67. Costume
68. Girl
69. Handle
70. Nautilus
71. Vigilance
72. Figurehead
73. Ace
74. Kilowatt
75. Skipper
76. Persuasion
77. Compound
78. Sideline
79. Paint
80. Inventory
81. Cement
82. Summation
83. Megaphone
84. User
85. Murmur
86. Dad
87. Fruit
88. Complainant
89. Thesis
90. Importer
91. Age
92. Plug
93. Committee
94. Mussel
95. Separatist
96. Whoop
97. Mahogany
98. Stockpile
99. Manipulation

0. Instinct
1. Endorsement
2. Cow
3. Wigwam
4. Combination
5. Emergence
6. Cosine
7. Foreword
8. Most
9. Pundit
10. Dunce
11. Tavern
12. Pivot
13. Belly
14. Strand
15. Consequence
16. Scribbler
17. Jotting
18. Operator
19. Violet
20. Clip
21. Potpourri
22. Payment
23. Placebo
24. Spoils
25. Jay
26. Singularity
27. Aquarium
28. Prelude
29. Cherry
30. Notepaper
31. Sunflower
32. Island
33. Cord
34. Postponement
35. Coordinates
36. Spiral
37. Undertaker
38. Poacher
39. Wanton
40. Listener
41. Cluck
42. Ratchet
43. Rice
44. Wording
45. Retriever
46. Repentance
47. Octagon
48. Start
49. Prospectus
50. Adjustment
51. Holiness
52. Terrapin
53. Viewpoint
54. Fierceness
55. Trunk
56. Osprey
57. Spoonful
58. Classification
59. Acupuncture
60. Nutriment
61. Oddity
62. Incision
63. Plot
64. Alien
65. Estuary
66. Cheetah
67. Reproduction
68. Vigil
69. Tendril
70. Goldfinch
71. Miller
72. Deposition
73. Kindliness
74. Tinker
75. Burlap
76. Shanty
77. Teaching
78. Slap
79. Headband
80. Syndrome
81. Beef
82. Women
83. Compartment
84. Sedation
85. Cyclone
86. Clash
87. Compote
88. Stratum
89. Boot
90. Conspiracy
91. Revolutionary
92. Testimonial
93. Druid
94. Slalom
95. Catkin
96. Drawers
97. Statue
98. Protagonist
99. Skateboarding

0. Flurry	34. Key	68. Pride
1. Bodkin	35. Spokesperson	69. Influence
2. Negation	36. Register	70. Stray
3. Hamburger	37. Grille	71. Generalization
4. Warlock	38. Teaser	72. Blunder
5. Tail	39. Sinner	73. Cotton
6. Advice	40. Scissors	74. Banker
7. Punishment	41. Temperature	75. Clientele
8. Sprite	42. Brandy	76. Sidekick
9. Kiosk	43. Stew	77. Bow
10. Loofah	44. Snowcap	78. Election
11. Widower	45. Aptitude	79. Hysterics
12. Dispensary	46. Penthouse	80. Loot
13. Sorrel	47. Horse	81. Castaway
14. Draftsman	48. Pillow	82. Summit
15. Brace	49. Respiration	83. Seven
16. Emotion	50. Shovel	84. Accompaniment
17. Maize	51. Lexicographer	85. Cruiser
18. Marjoram	52. Thumb	86. Inland
19. Saturday	53. Birch	87. Heaven
20. Nepotism	54. Tamale	88. Toothbrush
21. Tautology	55. Upstate	89. Gunfire
22. Hairnet	56. Austerity	90. Dishwasher
23. Sword	57. Product	91. Cowgirl
24. Pantomime	58. Shepherdess	92. Thicket
25. Concrete	59. Heathen	93. Ox
26. Ingot	60. Milkman	94. Purse
27. Officialdom	61. Cash	95. Fib
28. Market	62. Matchmaker	96. Keeper
29. Diction	63. Creature	97. Packing
30. Magistrate	64. Atonement	98. Thirteenth
31. Flattery	65. Deity	99. Pension
32. Fixture	66. Enormity	
33. Blare	67. Insecurity	

0. Pontoon	34. Trouble	68. Bus
1. Zest	35. Wedding	69. Hostel
2. Spyglass	36. Scaremonger	70. Gunrunning
3. Rug	37. Attendee	71. Review
4. Altar	38. Repute	72. Eternity
5. Beagle	39. Curfew	73. Voltage
6. Cheat	40. Handcart	74. Rout
7. Receipt	41. Fitter	75. Cursor
8. Mishap	42. Tempest	76. Proficiency
9. Gangway	43. Scout	77. Pith
10. Pond	44. Ethics	78. Coat
11. Ridge	45. Moth	79. Concession
12. Standby	46. Fruitcake	80. Salesman
13. Teddy	47. Government	81. Heartache
14. Beacon	48. Shipment	82. Stair
15. Theology	49. Wiener	83. Scabbard
16. Boulder	50. Billboard	84. Ship
17. Snatch	51. Footstool	85. Abdication
18. Airfield	52. Locust	86. Drain
19. Turbine	53. Brew	87. Incident
20. Happiness	54. Scholar	88. Whiz
21. Chlorine	55. Banner	89. Psychologist
22. Haw	56. Dud	90. Petroleum
23. Canoe	57. Babysitter	91. Convector
24. Smokehouse	58. Craftsmanship	92. Gin
25. Minnow	59. Weakling	93. Stratagem
26. Frog	60. Varnish	94. Councilor
27. Poncho	61. Circumstance	95. Tranquilizer
28. Racehorse	62. Wheelwright	96. Consort
29. Fossil	63. Century	97. Might
30. Rosemary	64. Humus	98. Messenger
31. Shire	65. Cello	99. Dogcart
32. Chicken	66. Cobblestone	
33. Span	67. Cushion	

0. Backgammon	34. Drake	68. Froth
1. Finesse	35. Overalls	69. Thrush
2. Squall	36. Location	70. Ocean
3. Depletion	37. Orifice	71. Mellowness
4. Nightfall	38. Embassy	72. Implement
5. Orgy	39. Gouge	73. Tern
6. Primacy	40. Steamship	74. Country
7. Joviality	41. Scone	75. Reputation
8. Suggestion	42. Mace	76. Hardball
9. Stimulus	43. Predator	77. Reverse
10. Cooperation	44. Drip	78. Plait
11. Constable	45. Broom	79. Countenance
12. Windfall	46. Baton	80. Sled
13. Deserter	47. Carol	81. Cause
14. Declaration	48. Cravat	82. Backhand
15. Luster	49. Drift	83. Fallibility
16. Deportment	50. Hawk	84. Reed
17. Aviary	51. Scepter	85. Bustle
18. Acoustics	52. Patter	86. Eventuality
19. Conference	53. Wriggle	87. Dredge
20. Haricot	54. Fake	88. Night
21. Bazaar	55. Token	89. Contraband
22. Conjecture	56. Feedback	90. Car
23. Utilitarian	57. Insistence	91. Headland
24. Helium	58. Agreement	92. Inhumanity
25. Zebra	59. Supremacist	93. Denominator
26. Tutor	60. Prevention	94. Date
27. Voluntary	61. Beachcomber	95. Aid
28. Siesta	62. Blot	96. Sailer
29. Netherworld	63. Tandoori	97. Sixteen
30. Material	64. Fish	98. Agriculture
31. Tricycle	65. Scraping	99. Hemline
32. Peace	66. Sewage	
33. Accident	67. Asphalt	

0. Icing	34. Wrangler	68. Nuance
1. Pup	35. Curiosity	69. Severity
2. Spender	36. Offering	70. Pop
3. Chirp	37. Shuttle	71. Pugnacity
4. Tiptoe	38. Stablemate	72. Yank
5. Excursion	39. Pudding	73. Hotbed
6. Indigo	40. Submarine	74. Squint
7. Spume	41. Prostration	75. Bother
8. Adulteration	42. Ranger	76. Pounce
9. Hearer	43. Museum	77. Precaution
10. Credentials	44. Mess	78. Emulation
11. Arrest	45. Lad	79. Lapse
12. Metabolism	46. Center	80. Derailment
13. Vole	47. Trace	81. Surfboard
14. Frankness	48. Horseradish	82. Doldrums
15. Satyr	49. Policewoman	83. Contract
16. Current	50. Dictatorship	84. Regiment
17. Cosmos	51. Tenure	85. Inversion
18. Microchip	52. Pity	86. Alarmist
19. Myrtle	53. Gondolier	87. Love
20. Droop	54. Qualm	88. Team
21. Tinder	55. Buffalo	89. Manhood
22. Hurry	56. Iron	90. Foundation
23. Discussion	57. Bravado	91. Clot
24. Crisis	58. College	92. Pillowcase
25. Benefit	59. Billiards	93. Minute
26. Astrology	60. Dampness	94. Aunt
27. Drapery	61. Pick	95. Diffuse
28. Connection	62. Pot	96. Broth
29. Inhalation	63. Mercy	97. Lodging
30. Saunter	64. Wag	98. Lily
31. Borrower	65. Sheath	99. Strategist
32. White	66. Convertible	
33. Hurdle	67. Default	

<table>
<tr><td>0. Splat</td><td>34. Nursing</td><td>68. Chancellor</td></tr>
<tr><td>1. Snowboarding</td><td>35. Safeguard</td><td>69. Movement</td></tr>
<tr><td>2. Tycoon</td><td>36. Sale</td><td>70. Sassafras</td></tr>
<tr><td>3. Allegiance</td><td>37. Sinker</td><td>71. Goodwill</td></tr>
<tr><td>4. Human</td><td>38. Panther</td><td>72. Diameter</td></tr>
<tr><td>5. Pliancy</td><td>39. Version</td><td>73. Ape</td></tr>
<tr><td>6. Outline</td><td>40. Trick</td><td>74. Gum</td></tr>
<tr><td>7. Yoke</td><td>41. Financier</td><td>75. Hockey</td></tr>
<tr><td>8. Seasoning</td><td>42. Strut</td><td>76. Horde</td></tr>
<tr><td>9. Gulp</td><td>43. Fisherman</td><td>77. Housework</td></tr>
<tr><td>10. Numerator</td><td>44. Arithmetic</td><td>78. Devil</td></tr>
<tr><td>11. Brunette</td><td>45. Sonar</td><td>79. Runway</td></tr>
<tr><td>12. Gel</td><td>46. Posterity</td><td>80. Subject</td></tr>
<tr><td>13. Manila</td><td>47. Headspring</td><td>81. Fender</td></tr>
<tr><td>14. Hairdresser</td><td>48. Elastic</td><td>82. Budget</td></tr>
<tr><td>15. Reconsideration</td><td>49. Refutation</td><td>83. Diversity</td></tr>
<tr><td>16. Acceptance</td><td>50. Dusk</td><td>84. Gesture</td></tr>
<tr><td>17. Patent</td><td>51. Iridescence</td><td>85. Lounge</td></tr>
<tr><td>18. Noun</td><td>52. Liniment</td><td>86. Knell</td></tr>
<tr><td>19. Cutback</td><td>53. Vertigo</td><td>87. Monolog</td></tr>
<tr><td>20. Towel</td><td>54. Greenery</td><td>88. Trestle</td></tr>
<tr><td>21. Concept</td><td>55. Sharp</td><td>89. Therapy</td></tr>
<tr><td>22. Donor</td><td>56. Dissection</td><td>90. Machete</td></tr>
<tr><td>23. Trustee</td><td>57. Malice</td><td>91. Hailstone</td></tr>
<tr><td>24. Police</td><td>58. Cabin</td><td>92. Zither</td></tr>
<tr><td>25. Header</td><td>59. Thunderstorm</td><td>93. Gear</td></tr>
<tr><td>26. Lariat</td><td>60. Minstrel</td><td>94. Heartbeat</td></tr>
<tr><td>27. Scoop</td><td>61. Convocation</td><td>95. Reasoning</td></tr>
<tr><td>28. Lynx</td><td>62. Evolution</td><td>96. Wing</td></tr>
<tr><td>29. Replica</td><td>63. Soapbox</td><td>97. Relief</td></tr>
<tr><td>30. Author</td><td>64. Distraction</td><td>98. Tweak</td></tr>
<tr><td>31. Diversion</td><td>65. Doublet</td><td>99. Gray</td></tr>
<tr><td>32. Toss</td><td>66. Barmaid</td><td></td></tr>
<tr><td>33. Paprika</td><td>67. Radon</td><td></td></tr>
</table>

0. Philologist
1. Balance
2. Mobile
3. Account
4. Juniper
5. Marcher
6. Flatterer
7. Quandary
8. Epilog
9. Heave
10. Poverty
11. Thunder
12. Battalion
13. Membership
14. Connotation
15. Fallacy
16. Geniality
17. Tuna
18. Traveler
19. Suffering
20. Wallet
21. Expatriate
22. Ivy
23. Employee
24. Fumigant
25. Neck
26. Trademark
27. Dragonfly
28. Reunion
29. Magnate
30. Pail
31. Twinkle
32. Millipede
33. Recoil
34. Dust
35. Teens
36. Chandelier
37. Halt
38. Wednesday
39. Envoy
40. Tenderness
41. Constitution
42. Taste
43. Loaf
44. Haven
45. Periodical
46. Sea
47. Inevitability
48. Reflex
49. Coast
50. Touchiness
51. Panic
52. Bachelor
53. Container
54. Necktie
55. Grasshopper
56. Wait
57. Sunglasses
58. Sorcery
59. Clog
60. Stairway
61. Percussion
62. Contrast
63. Kitbag
64. Swindler
65. Use
66. Unconformity
67. Move
68. Trinity
69. Disuse
70. Homonym
71. Fly
72. Entreaty
73. Fact
74. Sprinkle
75. Herring
76. Snow
77. Stature
78. Sensitivity
79. Detachment
80. Uncertainty
81. Inch
82. Attitude
83. Valet
84. Peeress
85. Station
86. Reinforcements
87. Attempt
88. Likeness
89. Earshot
90. Mane
91. Accomplishment
92. Sallow
93. Cider
94. Banality
95. Fern
96. Ragtime
97. Deflection
98. Goblet
99. Goblin

0. Climber
1. Beaker
2. Hundred
3. Shadow
4. Soporific
5. Watershed
6. Nan
7. Pageantry
8. Megabyte
9. Sparkle
10. Trigonometry
11. Forth
12. Brother
13. Minefield
14. Tic
15. Moor
16. Chattel
17. Bud
18. Melancholy
19. Collie
20. Idealism
21. Hulk
22. Yesterday
23. Schedule
24. Snip
25. Contour
26. Gallon
27. Slipper
28. Armament
29. Message
30. List
31. Cork
32. Exploration
33. Precedent
34. Legend
35. Cape
36. Probe
37. Yacht
38. Juror
39. Invincibility
40. Order
41. District
42. Trader
43. Sap
44. Salvation
45. Dead
46. Saguaro
47. Zoologist
48. Two
49. Coyote
50. Middleman
51. Rattle
52. Mildew
53. Raid
54. Impulsiveness
55. Firmness
56. Mastiff
57. Farmstead
58. Craft
59. Avocado
60. League
61. Conjuncture
62. Gash
63. Hostility
64. Clue
65. Knob
66. Yeti
67. Baronet
68. Finding
69. Quarterback
70. View
71. Scourings
72. Flauta
73. Catapult
74. Plan
75. Fairy
76. Finish
77. Effeminacy
78. Mat
79. Mob
80. Amazement
81. South
82. Rubber
83. Stole
84. Canteen
85. Velocity
86. Proposal
87. Agate
88. Width
89. Marauder
90. Corduroy
91. Topping
92. Contempt
93. Modem
94. Shackles
95. Protectionist
96. Residency
97. Wipe
98. Tackle
99. Desperation

0. Mobility	34. Spectator	68. Respirator
1. Sampan	35. Housing	69. Gig
2. Fervor	36. Stinger	70. Shotgun
3. Sharif	37. Glutton	71. Trillion
4. Clamor	38. School	72. Abbreviation
5. Anthem	39. County	73. Total
6. Exclusion	40. Cleaner	74. Brim
7. Chute	41. Shrew	75. Elongation
8. Maxim	42. Lash	76. Diet
9. Casino	43. Roost	77. Decency
10. Oath	44. Metallurgist	78. Investment
11. Homeowner	45. Deportation	79. Circuit
12. Replacement	46. Odyssey	80. Prune
13. Portraiture	47. Executive	81. Tea
14. Tails	48. Outdoors	82. Machine
15. Lump	49. Sticker	83. Representative
16. Graft	50. Assumption	84. Cavern
17. Conveyance	51. Cygnet	85. Prospect
18. Garage	52. Midwinter	86. Battlement
19. Lupin	53. Disease	87. Mouthpiece
20. Pigeon	54. Quack	88. Articulation
21. Navigator	55. Husbandry	89. Balloon
22. Catalog	56. Frill	90. Oxidation
23. Requirement	57. Trickery	91. Windshield
24. Producer	58. Dryness	92. Papyrus
25. Hypocrisy	59. Watch	93. Clod
26. Beach	60. Wont	94. Die
27. Storage	61. Forestation	95. Hydraulics
28. Dormer	62. Shaft	96. Epic
29. Crease	63. Dullness	97. Tissue
30. Meditation	64. Mansion	98. Baby
31. Incorporation	65. Meanness	99. Pursuer
32. Lilt	66. Blow	
33. Bail	67. Tadpole	

0. Revocation	34. Jazz	68. Landlord
1. Bell	35. Lick	69. Stipulation
2. Penance	36. Hero	70. Pitcher
3. Perm	37. Possibility	71. Villa
4. Strait	38. Physics	72. Spotlight
5. Handoff	39. Fleck	73. Solo
6. Snowdrift	40. Polo	74. Belief
7. Caste	41. Convenience	75. Nimbleness
8. Lay	42. Realty	76. Pocket
9. Gore	43. Rhombus	77. Pinnacle
10. Neckerchief	44. Manor	78. Spare
11. Checkers	45. Antecedents	79. Volume
12. Creed	46. Parasite	80. Whiskey
13. Jackass	47. Kale	81. Homemade
14. Courtier	48. Freckle	82. Garb
15. Surge	49. Friend	83. Distortion
16. Rule	50. Carp	84. Variety
17. Fathom	51. Fellowship	85. Television
18. Attraction	52. Discount	86. Warehouse
19. Bullfrog	53. Shortage	87. Hate
20. Ankle	54. Clerk	88. Canopy
21. Sanctity	55. Profanity	89. Calico
22. Connivance	56. Border	90. Terror
23. Pastry	57. Chalice	91. Anxiety
24. Palisade	58. Starlet	92. Philanthropy
25. Internment	59. Purl	93. Splice
26. Jealousy	60. Flannel	94. Amigo
27. Marquee	61. Mirth	95. Survival
28. Fishmonger	62. Vagabond	96. Description
29. Dumps	63. Lead	97. Individual
30. Embodiment	64. Libertine	98. Opinion
31. Mathematics	65. Fixation	99. Lawn
32. Server	66. Fjord	
33. Bloom	67. Khaki	

0. Twilight	34. Torrent	68. Aqueduct
1. Speaker	35. Terracotta	69. Broadness
2. Minority	36. Textbook	70. Morning
3. Disapproval	37. Bluebell	71. Hut
4. Satay	38. Fullback	72. Covenant
5. Hand	39. Session	73. Cat
6. Belfry	40. Soccer	74. Zinc
7. Motel	41. Federation	75. Flour
8. Truant	42. Fundraiser	76. Biography
9. Element	43. Puritanism	77. Lifebelt
10. Plethora	44. Energy	78. Yowl
11. Caricature	45. Lawnmower	79. Today
12. Slant	46. Ordinance	80. Imagination
13. Minus	47. Beard	81. Hack
14. Depot	48. Handsaw	82. Passenger
15. Sky	49. Allergy	83. Commander
16. Ampersand	50. Obsession	84. Parsnip
17. Stepfather	51. Tailgate	85. Finality
18. Tramp	52. Distiller	86. Renown
19. Masseuse	53. Whey	87. Technique
20. Drawl	54. Drugstore	88. Shriek
21. Crony	55. Brief	89. Crow
22. Swordfish	56. Ginger	90. Naturalist
23. Lance	57. Fashion	91. Gang
24. Ear	58. Performer	92. Preparation
25. Animation	59. Pewter	93. Spit
26. Wager	60. Outback	94. Clarinet
27. Blizzard	61. Simplicity	95. Fife
28. Pampas	62. Privation	96. Fastener
29. February	63. Housekeeper	97. Drop
30. Engraving	64. Mode	98. Compendium
31. Insignia	65. Primer	99. Swing
32. Drink	66. Toil	
33. Saucepan	67. Jitters	

0. Jonquil
1. Discretion
2. Concord
3. Significance
4. Deadlock
5. Cryptic
6. Blazer
7. Noose
8. Flap
9. Snowshoe
10. Ruler
11. Groundskeeper
12. Spacecraft
13. Arrogance
14. Danger
15. Interruption
16. Saint
17. Burner
18. Ventilator
19. Loafer
20. Ammonia
21. Woodworm
22. Hairstyle
23. Coincidence
24. Authority
25. Sesame
26. Belongings
27. Comprehension
28. Misfit
29. Criticism
30. Plate
31. Speedboat
32. Nurture
33. Imposition
34. Spice
35. Priory
36. Hangar
37. Look
38. Charm
39. Potato
40. Dollar
41. Bride
42. Jump
43. Hiatus
44. Downfall
45. Section
46. Vault
47. Inflexibility
48. Spear
49. Size
50. Chart
51. Chemistry
52. Slice
53. Widow
54. Stopwatch
55. Gurgle
56. Palmist
57. Stutter
58. Septuplet
59. Weirdness
60. Pace
61. Dolor
62. Embargo
63. Brotherhood
64. Exception
65. Flipper
66. Alley
67. Sanity
68. Satellite
69. Figure
70. Egoist
71. Store
72. Dictation
73. Poise
74. Suburb
75. Dynamo
76. Barter
77. Flag
78. Introduction
79. Ozone
80. Mortification
81. Coating
82. Hedgehog
83. Nettle
84. Mire
85. Mania
86. Cannon
87. Premeditation
88. Dice
89. Zenith
90. Traditional
91. Bicentennial
92. Bind
93. Ladder
94. Counterpart
95. Urn
96. University
97. Soul
98. Absorption
99. Wall

0. Accumulation
1. Groundwork
2. Pragmatism
3. Ingrowth
4. Tutorial
5. Relaxation
6. Douche
7. Nose
8. Stepchild
9. Sketch
10. Sailing
11. Protector
12. Explanation
13. Proof
14. Brisket
15. Merriment
16. Pavement
17. Manatee
18. Drawing
19. Speedometer
20. Solidarity
21. Defiance
22. Ruse
23. Plaything
24. Juxtaposition
25. Wicket
26. Camisole
27. Ban
28. Batch
29. Headlock
30. Anticlimax
31. Dramatist
32. Combatant
33. Ally
34. Canal
35. Playhouse
36. Excitement
37. Culinary
38. Extreme
39. Cast
40. Detainee
41. Busybody
42. Vanilla
43. Vulture
44. Fickleness
45. Attainment
46. Jumpiness
47. Leap
48. Monolith
49. Way
50. Reign
51. Cry
52. Retraction
53. Tint
54. Camp
55. Calorie
56. Maximum
57. Matchbox
58. Halibut
59. Spike
60. Northwest
61. Third
62. Dresser
63. Vase
64. Miser
65. Sexism
66. Wagtail
67. Ire
68. Manifesto
69. Orator
70. Corruption
71. Diagnosis
72. Horoscope
73. Jollity
74. Metropolis
75. Crib
76. Blur
77. Referee
78. Thanks
79. Idiocy
80. Illness
81. Probity
82. Hunk
83. Chauvinist
84. Vigor
85. Terminal
86. Lioness
87. Water
88. Dean
89. Dermatologist
90. Wattage
91. Pedestrian
92. Tally
93. Misanthrope
94. Flame
95. Steamboat
96. Specialist
97. Conic
98. Bracelet
99. Coinage

0. Immoralist	34. Rover	68. Pretender
1. Reconstruction	35. Immorality	69. Lemur
2. Colt	36. Legibility	70. Mantle
3. Modicum	37. Constellation	71. Radiologist
4. Trousers	38. Lough	72. Suffix
5. Tour	39. Self	73. Henna
6. Diamond	40. Burst	74. Schoolwork
7. Dominoes	41. Potassium	75. General
8. Reptile	42. Talisman	76. Wrath
9. Portico	43. Jeer	77. Examinee
10. Department	44. Reception	78. Ailment
11. Flick	45. Normality	79. Nectar
12. Efficiency	46. Fry	80. Wreath
13. Impartiality	47. Law	81. Breeding
14. Tuesday	48. Security	82. Amoeba
15. Shoal	49. Slogan	83. Blacklist
16. Kind	50. Glimmer	84. Teenager
17. Freshwater	51. Discharge	85. Hopscotch
18. Monogamist	52. Muskrat	86. Tornado
19. Racketeer	53. Peanut	87. Confines
20. Lip	54. Fiddle	88. Mullion
21. Theatricals	55. Roundabout	89. Successor
22. Tardiness	56. Symptom	90. Pile
23. Baggage	57. Samurai	91. Hodgepodge
24. Adapter	58. Righteousness	92. Loss
25. Violinist	59. Escalator	93. Prototype
26. Flamenco	60. Affliction	94. Fool
27. Scorcher	61. Daisy	95. Underfur
28. Load	62. Bloodshed	96. Court
29. Secularity	63. Meteor	97. Backyard
30. Gutter	64. Detective	98. Follower
31. Critique	65. Hoard	99. Tank
32. Series	66. Knighthood	
33. Shingle	67. Disturbance	

0. Mastery	34. Cranberry	68. Leniency
1. Tradesperson	35. Hornet	69. Headmaster
2. Pet	36. Pacifist	70. Revel
3. Wobble	37. Propeller	71. Woodcut
4. Shopkeeper	38. Culture	72. Musket
5. Wheel	39. Caretaker	73. Trident
6. Cheer	40. Mythology	74. Refrain
7. Fourteen	41. Opossum	75. Counterattack
8. Reggae	42. Brand	76. Tambourine
9. Motorist	43. Designation	77. Greyhound
10. Electronics	44. Evil	78. Custard
11. Mimicry	45. Shortcake	79. Caster
12. Psychic	46. Expedience	80. Improvement
13. Lab	47. Charcoal	81. Radiographer
14. Shack	48. Mate	82. Abductor
15. Grandson	49. Spiritualism	83. Heartsease
16. Stirrup	50. Ammunition	84. Duke
17. Swell	51. Barbarity	85. Headdress
18. Contention	52. Truancy	86. Motherhood
19. Assets	53. Houri	87. Bath
20. Prairie	54. Barley	88. Whirlwind
21. Enthronement	55. Stampede	89. Coach
22. Copyright	56. Marathon	90. Tragedy
23. Restoration	57. Focus	91. Graduation
24. Reformation	58. Deterrent	92. Discipline
25. Rally	59. Believer	93. Visage
26. Tiller	60. Gag	94. Guess
27. Adornment	61. Twitch	95. Scrim
28. Candle	62. Stagnation	96. Offshoot
29. Idiom	63. Bubble	97. Hail
30. Boy	64. Stockade	98. Stronghold
31. Inclination	65. Hexagon	99. Prank
32. Atlas	66. Native	
33. Threat	67. Stake	

0. Indignation	34. Viola	68. Clearance
1. Bearing	35. Pupa	69. Lake
2. Proximity	36. Finger	70. Clergy
3. Heath	37. Rabbit	71. Crank
4. End	38. Gossip	72. Minion
5. Octet	39. Waltz	73. Carver
6. Cinema	40. Knife	74. Round
7. Marquetry	41. Bibliophile	75. Hunch
8. Door	42. Clothing	76. Observer
9. Faucet	43. Discrepancy	77. Paperback
10. Sass	44. Spoof	78. Pants
11. Disciplinarian	45. Novitiate	79. Bliss
12. Readership	46. Hug	80. Qualification
13. Discord	47. Template	81. Stalactite
14. Harmonica	48. Nectarine	82. Roe
15. Ornithologist	49. Jolt	83. Detonator
16. Morsel	50. Punt	84. Constitutional
17. Dryad	51. Verb	85. Detail
18. Broiler	52. Oil	86. Ledge
19. Rider	53. Gargle	87. Handprint
20. Rhyme	54. Sierra	88. Insect
21. Mimosa	55. Piano	89. Dandy
22. Acrobat	56. Havoc	90. Volley
23. Interest	57. Miss	91. Signage
24. Sedition	58. Shape	92. Stare
25. Inset	59. Mosque	93. Military
26. Gorilla	60. Liquidation	94. Ecology
27. Selection	61. Scanner	95. Bedrock
28. Entertainment	62. Recess	96. Coquette
29. Roebuck	63. Pie	97. Rigmarole
30. Frankfurter	64. Rouge	98. Naught
31. Cultivation	65. Year	99. Felony
32. Diversification	66. Whine	
33. Backpack	67. Tangle	

0. Whiting	34. Revivalist	68. Itch
1. Melon	35. Shout	69. Capability
2. Penmanship	36. Motto	70. Cavalry
3. Nickel	37. Spot	71. Specter
4. Thanksgiving	38. Secessionist	72. Floss
5. Upset	39. Saltshaker	73. Despondency
6. Smorgasbord	40. Cod	74. Frequency
7. Anthology	41. Trumpet	75. Flashcard
8. Twister	42. Granule	76. Touchstone
9. Bulk	43. Imperfection	77. Sycamore
10. Neutral	44. Inn	78. Vinegar
11. Garment	45. Redundancy	79. Incredulity
12. China	46. Meteorite	80. Oven
13. Eaves	47. Odor	81. Eradication
14. Refuse	48. Pennant	82. Insincerity
15. Percent	49. Latchkey	83. Branch
16. Cock	50. Economy	84. Cordiality
17. Moat	51. Manifestation	85. Graveyard
18. Pallor	52. Carat	86. Filling
19. Interstate	53. Nostalgia	87. Epaulette
20. Distributor	54. Engineering	88. Parson
21. Marshmallow	55. Magnification	89. Consultation
22. Regulator	56. Battle	90. Pharmacist
23. Cardboard	57. Germ	91. Dedication
24. Pledge	58. Enemy	92. Glorification
25. Orientation	59. Amnesia	93. Sexuality
26. Nit	60. Radiology	94. Person
27. Insolence	61. Booby	95. Lair
28. Liner	62. Motor	96. Hansom
29. Front	63. Hotshot	97. Freezer
30. Centipede	64. Legislation	98. Sleeve
31. Cinnamon	65. Interpretation	99. Kite
32. Stump	66. Trade	
33. Companion	67. Nausea	

0. Trainee	34. Pyramid	68. Linoleum
1. Bait	35. Bite	69. Teak
2. Trigger	36. Indirection	70. Assortment
3. Parchment	37. Flavor	71. Physiologist
4. Liability	38. Millet	72. Acronym
5. Disappointment	39. Plum	73. Truck
6. Unit	40. Pothole	74. Blimp
7. Dispatch	41. Jury	75. Mummy
8. Theme	42. Happening	76. Shuttlecock
9. Three	43. Optimum	77. Yew
10. Clove	44. Packet	78. Appendicitis
11. Hope	45. Treaty	79. Voicemail
12. Chair	46. Maroon	80. Little
13. Intranet	47. Stamp	81. Tourist
14. Thyme	48. Birthmark	82. Emergency
15. Fling	49. Diner	83. Inadequacy
16. Sail	50. Shed	84. Whiff
17. Oats	51. Remission	85. Outing
18. Twelve	52. Archaism	86. Undergraduate
19. Hotel	53. Fuel	87. Photograph
20. Consonant	54. Contagion	88. Civilian
21. Heartsick	55. Enlargement	89. Effect
22. Gift	56. Turbulence	90. Jukebox
23. Veto	57. Fowl	91. Wickedness
24. Couplet	58. Coconut	92. Runner
25. Shipping	59. Birth	93. Pay
26. Bauble	60. Pylon	94. Heir
27. Caution	61. Adaptation	95. Usherette
28. Agency	62. Scent	96. Want
29. Gunpowder	63. Undergrowth	97. Anonymity
30. Avalanche	64. Woman	98. Stateswoman
31. Bangs	65. Narrative	99. Award
32. Mutineer	66. Shampoo	
33. Copper	67. Mortgage	

0. Restauranteur	34. Fuselage	68. Colonist
1. Tit	35. Sector	69. Shaving
2. Godchild	36. Viaduct	70. Plankton
3. Quartet	37. Bridegroom	71. Karaoke
4. Sunblock	38. Sleaze	72. Sepia
5. Sequoia	39. Outside	73. Pony
6. Accuracy	40. Injustice	74. Dramatization
7. Recluse	41. Mile	75. West
8. Singer	42. Tapir	76. Mystique
9. Evening	43. Neckline	77. Honeycomb
10. Installation	44. Parish	78. Simile
11. Say	45. Nobleman	79. Screen
12. Cleric	46. Autumn	80. Oboist
13. Landslide	47. Finalist	81. Hippo
14. Label	48. Prosody	82. Hump
15. Aviation	49. Loophole	83. Entrance
16. Pip	50. Handwriting	84. Commitment
17. Bib	51. Pawn	85. Ruffle
18. Driver	52. Regard	86. Moralist
19. Voucher	53. Zodiac	87. Kaleidoscope
20. Crayon	54. Meter	88. Aphorism
21. Spadework	55. Revue	89. Indentation
22. Solute	56. Infirmary	90. Terrorism
23. Acid	57. Opera	91. Increment
24. Slum	58. Cartography	92. Fireman
25. October	59. Survivalist	93. Admiral
26. Patio	60. Bull	94. Rising
27. Glance	61. Peeling	95. Announcement
28. Armistice	62. Clay	96. Loser
29. Lace	63. Beat	97. Popularity
30. Yodel	64. Tightrope	98. Secrecy
31. Wizardry	65. Dot	99. Term
32. Hallelujah	66. Hush	
33. Reel	67. Kitten	

0. Grip
1. Interrogation
2. Retaliation
3. Memorial
4. Elephant
5. Apex
6. Heredity
7. Echo
8. Sake
9. Instrumentation
10. Fortune
11. Diver
12. Taxi
13. Tennis
14. Candlestick
15. Levity
16. Ghetto
17. Matinee
18. Racketeering
19. Minimum
20. Comic
21. Periphery
22. Feeling
23. Bevy
24. Sable
25. Longing
26. Tell
27. Poison
28. Disgust
29. Whitewash
30. Eaglet
31. Sergeant
32. Captain
33. Promise
34. Communism
35. Seaboard
36. Stock
37. See
38. Asp
39. Secretary
40. Balsa
41. Trumpeter
42. Novice
43. Gazetteer
44. Dexterity
45. Vastness
46. Damage
47. Waterfall
48. Progress
49. Vernacular
50. Embezzlement
51. Fudge
52. Knock
53. Buttermilk
54. Diesel
55. Spurt
56. Fusion
57. Organization
58. Contact
59. Pod
60. Sitter
61. Ooze
62. Hummus
63. Debility
64. Tang
65. Incidence
66. Vibration
67. Cellulose
68. Sealant
69. Lunacy
70. Toddy
71. Entity
72. Rein
73. Foal
74. Wristwatch
75. Credibility
76. Motivation
77. Tureen
78. Yearling
79. Anthracite
80. Lender
81. Wreckage
82. Peddler
83. Vigilante
84. Heartbreak
85. Disadvantage
86. Dressing
87. Repeal
88. Girth
89. Environment
90. Dictionary
91. Guru
92. Matter
93. Assailant
94. Photo
95. Resurrection
96. Lingo
97. Bobbin
98. Planter
99. Dough

0. Quirk	34. Consulate	68. Stooge
1. Margin	35. Entirety	69. Leaflet
2. Platinum	36. Streetlight	70. Burden
3. Inference	37. Rye	71. Surplus
4. Osteopath	38. Interaction	72. Spearhead
5. Superstition	39. Obstacle	73. Revival
6. Extent	40. Stewardess	74. Binoculars
7. Peahen	41. Sentence	75. Islet
8. Lemming	42. Rupee	76. Pumice
9. Perennial	43. Gab	77. Municipality
10. Mahatma	44. Grandeur	78. Tout
11. Relative	45. Dowdiness	79. Topic
12. Disciple	46. Chigger	80. Sound
13. Spreadsheet	47. Quasar	81. Collective
14. Swish	48. Facsimile	82. Grease
15. Strain	49. Barracks	83. Brick
16. Sycophant	50. Conspirator	84. Deforestation
17. Prevalence	51. Practicality	85. Guarantee
18. Violation	52. Mobilization	86. Squelch
19. Model	53. Spree	87. Composure
20. Quest	54. Technicality	88. Owlet
21. Lattice	55. Gentleman	89. Defeat
22. Proportion	56. Judo	90. Friction
23. Evangelist	57. Longshoreman	91. Javelin
24. Plant	58. Vow	92. Sitar
25. Pilchard	59. Upbringing	93. Habit
26. Poultry	60. Pal	94. Contamination
27. Hayfield	61. Reach	95. Amiga
28. Lie	62. Crayfish	96. Affirmation
29. Jean	63. Bulrush	97. Portrait
30. Radiator	64. Initiative	98. Nonentity
31. Haft	65. Undershirt	99. Bump
32. Classic	66. Aggravation	
33. Fist	67. Gull	

0. Trimming	34. Lenience	68. Setup
1. Peculiarity	35. Nineteen	69. Motif
2. Kettle	36. Receptacle	70. Diaper
3. Alkali	37. Phantom	71. Suds
4. Catalyst	38. Boiler	72. Aridity
5. Nomination	39. Bulkhead	73. Establishment
6. Hilt	40. Lute	74. Lifetime
7. Distaste	41. Dial	75. Shrapnel
8. Lodger	42. Manicure	76. Robot
9. Migrant	43. Frenzy	77. Tannin
10. Predicament	44. Tiff	78. Frost
11. Swivel	45. Lotus	79. Residential
12. Pep	46. Specialty	80. Bikini
13. Set	47. Mockingbird	81. Insulation
14. Lighter	48. Nun	82. Rime
15. Needle	49. Taskmaster	83. Habitation
16. Guilt	50. Wilderness	84. Inscription
17. Dinosaur	51. Theory	85. Tap
18. Execution	52. Appliance	86. Rustle
19. Policy	53. Ditch	87. Gauntlet
20. Epoch	54. Gravitation	88. Discovery
21. Investigation	55. Dilation	89. Emanation
22. Waist	56. Lust	90. Asbestos
23. Tabulator	57. Winter	91. Stepmother
24. Chalet	58. Editorial	92. Rival
25. Parakeet	59. Camel	93. State
26. Triumvirate	60. Loathing	94. Slit
27. Boat	61. Thorn	95. Detour
28. Rabbi	62. Ego	96. Insecure
29. Wealth	63. Mention	97. Squirt
30. Sleepwalker	64. Buyer	98. Thinker
31. Slough	65. Verification	99. Genetics
32. Slip	66. Portion	
33. Marble	67. Varmint	

0. Snowboard
1. Nursemaid
2. Jester
3. Alignment
4. Troglodyte
5. Jellyfish
6. Workshop
7. Shekel
8. Interview
9. Justice
10. Regulation
11. Modernity
12. Watermark
13. Garrison
14. Suffocation
15. Heel
16. Euro
17. Approval
18. Titillation
19. Prey
20. Skateboard
21. Thimble
22. Trivia
23. Rebuttal
24. Sup
25. Mariner
26. Privilege
27. Horsefly
28. Haunt
29. Chancel
30. Tatters
31. Nephew
32. Python
33. Maharani
34. Accused
35. Goddess
36. Foyer
37. Wine
38. Crevice
39. Uncle
40. Principal
41. Satirist
42. Response
43. Undertow
44. Gentility
45. Grossness
46. Snobbery
47. Moose
48. Jigsaw
49. Observation
50. Islander
51. Mileage
52. Condition
53. Lettuce
54. Chieftain
55. Con
56. Weed
57. Stepdaughter
58. Reaper
59. Neurology
60. Emerald
61. Strip
62. Biochemistry
63. Illogic
64. Narwhal
65. Cave
66. Halftime
67. Clasp
68. Tuber
69. Monday
70. Scaffold
71. Dovetail
72. Bur
73. Lather
74. Colony
75. Inability
76. Stitch
77. Banjo
78. Impropriety
79. Freak
80. Starboard
81. Katydid
82. King
83. Seabird
84. Hangman
85. Adieu
86. Tassel
87. Primula
88. Marina
89. Pantyhose
90. Bracket
91. Laurel
92. Parallel
93. Wildfire
94. Duchy
95. Commemoration
96. Reserves
97. Warren
98. Commuter
99. Vocabulary

0. Intellectual	34. Parasang	68. Charioteer
1. Importation	35. Valley	69. Region
2. Textile	36. Cub	70. President
3. Health	37. Maze	71. Suspense
4. Gulch	38. Alarm	72. Materialist
5. Handstamp	39. Lineament	73. Navigation
6. Voyage	40. Wiper	74. Loam
7. Subtraction	41. Hertz	75. Criminal
8. Consumption	42. Tantrum	76. Superiority
9. Slapstick	43. Flaw	77. Prow
10. Intelligence	44. Lyrics	78. Discus
11. Quantum	45. Inventor	79. Buckle
12. Tenacity	46. Heater	80. Clatter
13. Analogy	47. Grin	81. Fugitive
14. Gunmetal	48. Exhibition	82. Scrap
15. Panacea	49. Pint	83. Glacier
16. Input	50. Individualism	84. Crown
17. Seamstress	51. Soap	85. Bowl
18. Rigor	52. Berry	86. Confetti
19. Friday	53. Commonwealth	87. Ingenuity
20. Risk	54. Waterworks	88. Proprietress
21. Extinction	55. Anesthetic	89. Robe
22. Lining	56. Personification	90. Rhubarb
23. Dig	57. Den	91. Fondness
24. Truism	58. Circulation	92. Visitor
25. Reliability	59. Poodle	93. Squash
26. Driblet	60. Irrelevancy	94. Wedlock
27. Hologram	61. Saddle	95. Furrow
28. Dozen	62. Peel	96. Tonne
29. Competitor	63. Lameness	97. Stretch
30. Property	64. Standpoint	98. Discomfort
31. Clink	65. Mission	99. Coup
32. Cuff	66. Watchmaker	
33. Leopard	67. Eligibility	

0. Missal
1. Jubilation
2. Invisibility
3. Misspelling
4. Fluke
5. Infusion
6. Romp
7. Bale
8. Rack
9. Book
10. Hindsight
11. Life
12. Babble
13. Woodpecker
14. Complaisance
15. Regency
16. Exhaust
17. Grater
18. Gladiator
19. Insanity
20. Site
21. Transom
22. Excellence
23. Microcosm
24. Vineyard
25. Challenge
26. Giraffe
27. Pug
28. Mortal
29. Balsam
30. Samba
31. Dairy
32. Clockwork
33. Chaps
34. Shading
35. Fennel
36. Fulfillment
37. Prosecutor
38. Leghorn
39. Pointer
40. Cruise
41. Banking
42. Sport
43. Infiltration
44. Fidelity
45. Cold
46. Hornpipe
47. Disagreement
48. Haddock
49. Fraternity
50. Margarine
51. Grammar
52. Spine
53. Lock
54. Pest
55. Lingerie
56. Enforcement
57. Unemployment
58. Netting
59. Retainer
60. Capacity
61. Balm
62. Demigod
63. Metallurgy
64. Pacification
65. Ocelot
66. Aloe
67. Garland
68. Roller
69. Sin
70. Green
71. Hobo
72. Gusto
73. Dwarf
74. Partridge
75. Senate
76. Bunker
77. Festival
78. Digression
79. Preview
80. Nutcracker
81. Lapdog
82. Irritability
83. Contralto
84. Ado
85. Endurance
86. Champion
87. Tortoise
88. Hunchback
89. Quadrangle
90. Respondent
91. Confederation
92. Earring
93. Dispersal
94. Misbehavior
95. Botany
96. Sire
97. Huddle
98. Fascination
99. Hazel

0. Flirtation
1. Cosmology
2. Ink
3. Usage
4. Natural
5. Immunology
6. Vocalist
7. Slipcase
8. Firewood
9. Hardness
10. Negligence
11. Billion
12. Tirade
13. Salary
14. Accolade
15. Satire
16. Draw
17. Autobiography
18. Spokeswoman
19. Turning
20. Novel
21. Livestock
22. Cover
23. Valediction
24. Invocation
25. Hessian
26. Hardtop
27. Parting
28. Nitwit
29. Pencil
30. Aspirin
31. Extrovert
32. Squadron
33. Spoon
34. Nip
35. Governess
36. Tension
37. Lantern
38. Gene
39. Exhaustion
40. Vale
41. Appraisal
42. Career
43. Till
44. Spook
45. Sandbag
46. Grog
47. Invention
48. Content
49. Crutch
50. Experiment
51. Pessimism
52. Misdemeanor
53. Caterer
54. Hurricane
55. Horn
56. Watt
57. Hull
58. Virtuoso
59. Trailer
60. Repair
61. Quarter
62. Flan
63. Necklace
64. Lumber
65. Destitution
66. Jewel
67. Bedding
68. Porpoise
69. Kidnapper
70. Kudos
71. Badger
72. Coexistence
73. Rotation
74. Religion
75. Toad
76. Cure
77. Stealth
78. Glamor
79. Frown
80. Shard
81. Electorate
82. Covering
83. Spaniel
84. Lyre
85. Reclamation
86. Leak
87. Downstate
88. Insignificance
89. Pasture
90. Accelerator
91. Anomaly
92. Breadth
93. Renewal
94. Graffiti
95. Disorganization
96. Godfather
97. Venue
98. Spinster
99. Bookworm

0. Trilogy
1. Agility
2. Calendar
3. Strategy
4. Constituent
5. Spunk
6. Dynamics
7. Thistle
8. Turntable
9. Grits
10. Amendment
11. Filings
12. Peasant
13. Blade
14. Grimace
15. Hallmark
16. Trickle
17. Biped
18. Need
19. Assassin
20. Brickbat
21. Wrapper
22. Integer
23. Magnesium
24. Surfeit
25. Skier
26. Exorcism
27. Prickle
28. Movie
29. Virtue
30. Wildlife
31. Citadel
32. Dumpling
33. Pottery
34. Beak
35. Dime
36. Invitation
37. Fund
38. Rummy
39. Untruth
40. Assembly
41. Barbecue
42. Miscellany
43. Quill
44. Terrace
45. Hangover
46. Carnation
47. Feudalism
48. Haste
49. Microbe
50. Prolongation
51. Pitch
52. Disrespect
53. Town
54. Palindrome
55. Eucalyptus
56. Citizen
57. Ford
58. Homeopathy
59. Intellect
60. Celery
61. Perfection
62. Grimness
63. Cordon
64. Hammerhead
65. Chase
66. Pit
67. Veranda
68. Bravery
69. Destiny
70. Stoic
71. Commerce
72. Frump
73. Fireworks
74. Asterisk
75. Cleanser
76. Convulsion
77. Beehive
78. Valency
79. Memoir
80. Duplication
81. Constriction
82. Passport
83. Sorority
84. Harelip
85. Serpent
86. Stall
87. Temptress
88. Toga
89. Piazza
90. Hatch
91. Insurer
92. Missionary
93. Shipyard
94. Algebra
95. Ugliness
96. Gadget
97. Bottom
98. Peal
99. Exclamation

0. Wrinkle	34. Traffic	68. Math
1. Proverb	35. Revision	69. Mesh
2. Dew	36. Palate	70. Foresight
3. Union	37. Monstrosity	71. Inferiority
4. Gelatin	38. Gasoline	72. Conscription
5. Deflation	39. Devaluation	73. Duality
6. Surrealism	40. Bargain	74. Outbreak
7. Income	41. Conjurer	75. Negotiator
8. Tick	42. Puritan	76. Jargon
9. Malformation	43. Lozenge	77. Lapel
10. Riches	44. Strength	78. Ferry
11. Amplifier	45. Malevolence	79. Tomboy
12. Batter	46. Rendition	80. Narrator
13. Tusk	47. Projection	81. Accommodation
14. Rivet	48. Adherence	82. Detergent
15. Success	49. Handrail	83. Printer
16. Plaque	50. Nanosecond	84. Agora
17. Fuzz	51. Automobile	85. Patient
18. Vine	52. Pistachio	86. Leggings
19. Underdog	53. Puberty	87. Stockbroker
20. Craving	54. Tsunami	88. Bread
21. Yardstick	55. Projectile	89. Augmentation
22. Immigrant	56. Demolition	90. Shamrock
23. Nozzle	57. Curb	91. Zeal
24. Individualist	58. Hind	92. Misuse
25. Handiness	59. Gentry	93. Sight
26. Abstract	60. Militiaman	94. Mutation
27. Strangeness	61. Serenade	95. Bee
28. Sequence	62. Denomination	96. Daytime
29. Stream	63. Scourge	97. Fourteenth
30. Excavator	64. Grievance	98. Typist
31. Yarn	65. Catamaran	99. Devilment
32. Specimen	66. Trawl	
33. Guts	67. Instrumentality	

0. Bystander	34. Sweater	68. Verdict
1. Espionage	35. Amethyst	69. Gaming
2. Outfield	36. Milkmaid	70. Chief
3. Odium	37. Padlock	71. Irony
4. Dock	38. Amateur	72. Counter
5. Currency	39. Swirl	73. Transept
6. Tire	40. Beeline	74. Butterscotch
7. Professional	41. Tulip	75. Cassock
8. Breast	42. Fluoride	76. Rear
9. Mineral	43. Folk	77. Database
10. Aphid	44. Steadiness	78. Custodian
11. Spinach	45. Direction	79. Smuggler
12. Immigration	46. Disservice	80. Chrysalis
13. Knot	47. Chaplain	81. Eighteen
14. Tone	48. Assertion	82. Pipes
15. Statistics	49. Wadding	83. Print
16. Viscosity	50. Smoker	84. Taco
17. Obelisk	51. Circlet	85. Brochure
18. Magistracy	52. Grandchild	86. Squeeze
19. Afternoon	53. Liberty	87. Jangle
20. Onrush	54. Cedar	88. Concentration
21. Intention	55. Onset	89. Kelp
22. Jab	56. Rejection	90. Tenor
23. Nap	57. Artifice	91. Shaker
24. Moisture	58. Regular	92. Rooster
25. Specs	59. Collusion	93. Incompetence
26. Juvenile	60. Insult	94. Quicksand
27. Scarlet	61. Recitation	95. Address
28. Protractor	62. Part	96. Southwest
29. Outset	63. Tenant	97. Emery
30. Spoiler	64. Piecework	98. Snap
31. Headroom	65. Fiddlehead	99. Oxymoron
32. Divergence	66. Condiment	
33. Stove	67. Hospital	

0. Protectorate	34. Quadrilateral	68. Medication
1. Creation	35. Trainer	69. Sidewalk
2. Settee	36. Honesty	70. Lecture
3. Freedom	37. Petrol	71. Linen
4. Remains	38. Screenplay	72. Hieroglyph
5. Larder	39. Well	73. Repertoire
6. Rot	40. Peak	74. Savoy
7. Hogwash	41. Wad	75. Zone
8. Squatter	42. Scorekeeper	76. Substitute
9. Calamity	43. Joint	77. Myrrh
10. Paragon	44. Terrier	78. Ratio
11. Expanse	45. Waitress	79. Firefighter
12. Gable	46. Asylum	80. Merger
13. Care	47. Cliff	81. Anatomy
14. Gallery	48. Allegro	82. Monogamy
15. Saleswoman	49. Angler	83. Imagery
16. Kill	50. Despair	84. Spatula
17. Virus	51. Stepson	85. Ply
18. Port	52. Incandescence	86. Backfire
19. Configuration	53. Goldfish	87. Square
20. Scarecrow	54. Embrace	88. Argument
21. Grandfather	55. Receptionist	89. Crystal
22. Kin	56. Filter	90. Pervert
23. Stoop	57. Mongoose	91. Rub
24. Fantasia	58. Festoon	92. Gunboat
25. Bench	59. Brook	93. Puff
26. Jot	60. Obligor	94. Complaint
27. Ohm	61. Wharf	95. Midriff
28. Anchor	62. Calculate	96. Clock
29. Paradise	63. Handstand	97. Shoplifter
30. Haul	64. Dove	98. Ensemble
31. Houseboat	65. Pulley	99. Hilltop
32. Admonition	66. Fate	
33. Cathedral	67. Taxation	

0. Dose
1. Client
2. Forklift
3. Pagoda
4. Plagiarist
5. Respect
6. Silt
7. Yore
8. Supernova
9. Goggles
10. Curtailment
11. Pajamas
12. Banish
13. Jaguar
14. Intrusion
15. Boyfriend
16. Actuality
17. Twill
18. Guava
19. Whirl
20. Speech
21. Sailor
22. Pineapple
23. Juggler
24. Encyclopedia
25. Auctioneer
26. Flock
27. Mason
28. Stepfamily
29. Cone
30. Quay
31. Criterion
32. Moleskin
33. Simper

34. Salutation
35. Venom
36. Preoccupation
37. Neighborhood
38. Balalaika
39. Mathematician
40. Stethoscope
41. Potion
42. Logbook
43. Disco
44. Tart
45. Deodorant
46. Cancellation
47. Gateway
48. Handbag
49. Understudy
50. Grab
51. Flue
52. Ascent
53. Guilder
54. Daredevil
55. Sibling
56. Pelican
57. Winner
58. Leadership
59. Fullness
60. Accordance
61. Press
62. Consonance
63. Fogey
64. Intersection
65. Men
66. Fable
67. Mouth

68. Moonbeam
69. Racket
70. Elf
71. Much
72. Snowmobile
73. Statement
74. Sense
75. Zoo
76. Regression
77. Bishop
78. Velour
79. Lecturer
80. Infatuation
81. Altitude
82. Nut
83. Foxhole
84. Lunch
85. Rush
86. Carrot
87. Gleam
88. Tar
89. Hamstring
90. Psychoanalyst
91. Volt
92. Squeak
93. Imprudence
94. Incinerator
95. Dandelion
96. Rod
97. Cellar
98. Tartar
99. Elevation

0. Yolk
1. Make
2. Charter
3. Canyon
4. Gusset
5. Coracle
6. Miter
7. Hubcap
8. Pulpit
9. Impertinence
10. Spell
11. Swine
12. Bore
13. Ninety
14. Hothead
15. Opacity
16. Purple
17. Egoism
18. Loan
19. Racoon
20. Ruble
21. Withers
22. Muslin
23. Passbook
24. Transistor
25. Tariff
26. Socialism
27. Privateer
28. Resumption
29. Utilitarianism
30. Depreciation
31. Linden
32. Expense
33. Fencing
34. Longbow
35. Serenity
36. Incarceration
37. Craze
38. Stupor
39. Midsummer
40. Umber
41. Conch
42. Idea
43. Blowtorch
44. Nomad
45. Rainwater
46. Linguist
47. Lateness
48. Methane
49. Cheddar
50. Saga
51. Franchise
52. Adjournment
53. Subsidy
54. Skirmish
55. Lintel
56. Quarry
57. Pant
58. Constabulary
59. Queen
60. Tense
61. Band
62. Halcyon
63. Cell
64. Breakage
65. Tetragon
66. Typescript
67. Omen
68. Trust
69. Newt
70. Smear
71. Technician
72. Ointment
73. Thatch
74. Ruby
75. Pellet
76. Dragon
77. Bent
78. Communion
79. Wedge
80. Tax
81. Sparsity
82. Idyll
83. Participation
84. Inhibition
85. Frontier
86. Nightcap
87. Risotto
88. Dispute
89. Drama
90. Spin
91. Dumbbells
92. Headmistress
93. Preterit
94. Croquet
95. Causeway
96. Audition
97. Wake
98. Nineteenth
99. Auditory

0. Barbarian	34. Moderate	68. Stack
1. Contraction	35. Grandstand	69. Bead
2. Credulity	36. Fright	70. Shebang
3. Senility	37. Chess	71. Timepiece
4. Adjective	38. Juncture	72. Headline
5. Crockery	39. Solid	73. Panorama
6. Stab	40. Devotion	74. Thursday
7. Sunday	41. Texture	75. Tip
8. Alligator	42. Jungle	76. Whisker
9. Contest	43. Extremist	77. Alert
10. Biographer	44. Commandment	78. Enthusiasm
11. Thrust	45. Extortion	79. Fount
12. Compact	46. Amplitude	80. Sweetening
13. Shag	47. Larva	81. Tribune
14. Splash	48. Prism	82. Jeopardy
15. Fuse	49. Left	83. Nominee
16. Deception	50. Kestrel	84. Mannequin
17. Uniform	51. Reference	85. Soot
18. Neutrality	52. Pensioner	86. Revolver
19. Juggernaut	53. Reviser	87. Thrashing
20. Emptiness	54. Jaywalker	88. Stiletto
21. Rhythm	55. Attire	89. Encounter
22. Vaccine	56. Ubiquity	90. Barrow
23. Essay	57. Possession	91. Industrialism
24. Womankind	58. Bastion	92. Yam
25. Slippage	59. Evidence	93. Duster
26. Corn	60. Laser	94. Interface
27. Rut	61. Marker	95. Antiquity
28. Psychology	62. Playmate	96. Volleyball
29. Washing	63. Aircraft	97. Grain
30. Hearsay	64. Firearm	98. Legion
31. Interplay	65. Recuperation	99. Magnet
32. Floor	66. Bunting	
33. Pole	67. Refrigeration	

0. Sandbar	34. Executioner	68. Remote
1. Supper	35. Coal	69. Honey
2. Midtown	36. Scrapbook	70. Barracuda
3. Millwheel	37. Orangutan	71. Wagon
4. Mainstream	38. Touch	72. Rapier
5. Smudge	39. Mainstay	73. Incentive
6. Cloth	40. Shadiness	74. Complex
7. Hag	41. Quesadilla	75. Nugget
8. Anthropology	42. Dogwatch	76. Milestone
9. Steak	43. Month	77. Flagpole
10. Desert	44. Husky	78. Average
11. Hound	45. Marketplace	79. Tenancy
12. Goat	46. Arsenic	80. Prose
13. Alimony	47. Christen	81. Parliament
14. Forerunner	48. Demeanor	82. Thunderbolt
15. Gold	49. Starlight	83. Roar
16. Stench	50. Teller	84. Sculpture
17. Silence	51. Shellac	85. Roughness
18. Lunge	52. Feed	86. Limitation
19. Ineptitude	53. Facilitation	87. Pseudonym
20. Tangent	54. Elaboration	88. Judgment
21. Creep	55. Chaos	89. Hoop
22. Furlong	56. Poetry	90. Eleventh
23. Snout	57. Indiscretion	91. Waste
24. Settle	58. Parentage	92. Controversy
25. Monotony	59. Rustler	93. Perspicacity
26. Procrastination	60. Pipeline	94. Saloon
27. Migration	61. Funnel	95. Hatter
28. Point	62. Reprieve	96. Hosanna
29. Headpiece	63. Shrubbery	97. Athletics
30. Crimson	64. Period	98. Landmark
31. Liar	65. Flamingo	99. Thought
32. Summons	66. Female	
33. Swig	67. Prettiness	

0. Stuffing
1. Petal
2. Verge
3. Remedy
4. Rainbow
5. Skate
6. Milk
7. Sway
8. Pool
9. Tab
10. Cripple
11. Thing
12. Atheist
13. Defendant
14. Boldness
15. Audibility
16. Antics
17. Puck
18. Query
19. Besom
20. Curling
21. Auditorium
22. Backwater
23. Impressionist
24. Homemaker
25. Technologist
26. Institution
27. Caucus
28. Jasmine
29. Substance
30. Circumference
31. Meeting
32. Handkerchief
33. Living
34. Fringe
35. Divisor
36. Rick
37. Rigidity
38. Hypnotist
39. Praise
40. Complication
41. Tradition
42. Mandate
43. East
44. Supply
45. Descent
46. Pen
47. Note
48. Falafel
49. Logo
50. Victor
51. Colonel
52. Punctuation
53. Respectability
54. Ejection
55. Subdivision
56. Artichoke
57. Metaphor
58. Moorhen
59. Addict
60. Tyrant
61. Satin
62. Speed
63. Cockpit
64. Mistress
65. Bat
66. Shorthorn
67. Refund
68. Metal
69. Kayak
70. Decathlon
71. Pedantry
72. Test
73. Trapdoor
74. Atrocity
75. Forestry
76. Easel
77. Crocus
78. Scrubland
79. Pocketbook
80. Prior
81. Pack
82. Grub
83. Limerick
84. Fit
85. Plotter
86. Double
87. Luck
88. Plural
89. Silica
90. Avarice
91. Healer
92. Sweetener
93. Equality
94. Swimwear
95. Basin
96. Abatement
97. Outfielder
98. Pump
99. Lipstick

0. Stonemason
1. Matrix
2. Console
3. Noble
4. Darkroom
5. Neckband
6. Comrade
7. Midget
8. Lob
9. Silverware
10. Ambassador
11. Grant
12. Uranus
13. Tongs
14. Speck
15. Pastille
16. Decision
17. Campaign
18. Greediness
19. Goose
20. Cutter
21. Identity
22. Barrel
23. Sump
24. Gentile
25. Submission
26. Mail
27. Authenticity
28. Pretext
29. Reek
30. Veteran
31. Pear
32. Protection
33. Spreader
34. Succotash
35. Sandstorm
36. Immediacy
37. Osteopathy
38. Holster
39. Evaporation
40. Casserole
41. Embroidery
42. Contribution
43. Guarantor
44. Helping
45. Snowdrop
46. Tome
47. Catch
48. Glint
49. Gluttony
50. Scribble
51. Strike
52. Sample
53. Marvel
54. Sacrifice
55. Coping
56. Accountant
57. Myopia
58. Patriarch
59. Bleach
60. Quicksilver
61. Tool
62. Youngster
63. Nude
64. Affection
65. Teaspoon
66. Nudge
67. Naturalism
68. Breakfast
69. Flashback
70. Tombstone
71. Cardigan
72. Biplane
73. Handset
74. Keeping
75. Snooker
76. Expurgation
77. Primate
78. Boss
79. Beeswax
80. Fitting
81. Reluctance
82. Smokestack
83. Virginity
84. Minuet
85. Raven
86. Permanence
87. Licorice
88. Stocking
89. One
90. Gradient
91. Brawler
92. Sleet
93. Convoy
94. Shuffleboard
95. Bondage
96. Trench
97. Disaster
98. Subtlety
99. Deletion

0. Flesh	34. Smirk	68. Socialist
1. Lyric	35. Subsistence	69. Herpetology
2. Dashboard	36. Grit	70. Bronze
3. Litter	37. Place	71. Bay
4. Lady	38. Emigrant	72. Mutilation
5. Profundity	39. Granite	73. Telescope
6. Narration	40. Cabbage	74. Transaction
7. Steeplechase	41. Medium	75. Potter
8. Plowman	42. Predilection	76. Fiasco
9. Boar	43. Cress	77. Amnesty
10. Economist	44. Bequest	78. Linseed
11. Endeavor	45. Valor	79. Tepee
12. Pygmy	46. Oracle	80. Piston
13. Upstairs	47. Squabble	81. Scallop
14. Gourd	48. Noodle	82. Assault
15. Broker	49. Reward	83. Pass
16. Carrier	50. Zipper	84. Subsidence
17. Recreation	51. Chain	85. Salvage
18. Beast	52. Canvas	86. Photographer
19. Acidity	53. Pan	87. Inhibitor
20. Album	54. Readjustment	88. Pioneer
21. Sandwich	55. Technology	89. Pretense
22. Peg	56. Abacus	90. Exasperation
23. Dog	57. Heirloom	91. Feather
24. Command	58. Clamp	92. Spillage
25. Ham	59. Daintiness	93. Accessibility
26. Peroxide	60. Rotunda	94. Boil
27. Witticism	61. Liberation	95. Hood
28. Exhilaration	62. Munitions	96. Stylistics
29. Colloquialism	63. Premise	97. Tableau
30. Snicker	64. Sawmill	98. Shimmer
31. Fascism	65. Ledger	99. Electrocution
32. Planetarium	66. Rescuer	
33. Concavity	67. Armory	

0. Darn	34. Delta	68. Giver
1. Celebration	35. Seniority	69. Totality
2. Informant	36. Foxhound	70. Smog
3. Lament	37. Fingernail	71. Bar
4. Stress	38. Core	72. Mascara
5. Nick	39. Otter	73. Rainforest
6. Arena	40. Faculty	74. Plasterer
7. Limber	41. Perspiration	75. Root
8. Purity	42. Atoll	76. Blanket
9. Bolt	43. Resistance	77. Wrist
10. Rapture	44. Wind	78. Attorney
11. Food	45. Slavery	79. Bomb
12. Nudity	46. Pull	80. Valentine
13. Meteorology	47. Panda	81. Steed
14. Porcupine	48. Fatality	82. Taint
15. Tango	49. Baptism	83. Muff
16. Acre	50. Sham	84. Cube
17. Correction	51. Voodoo	85. Hydroplane
18. Copse	52. Anathema	86. Background
19. Covert	53. Cornerstone	87. Nurse
20. Bookmaker	54. Ellipse	88. Waveband
21. Amalgamation	55. Visibility	89. Propagation
22. Breech	56. Seismology	90. Dress
23. Dustbin	57. Deficit	91. Ransom
24. Closet	58. Duress	92. Rupture
25. Leveret	59. Bridge	93. Burn
26. Dissolution	60. Finch	94. Totem
27. Ray	61. Extremity	95. Antenna
28. Crop	62. Stranger	96. Eruption
29. Godmother	63. Recipient	97. Adverb
30. Liqueur	64. Fillet	98. Heartstrings
31. Brilliance	65. Neighbor	99. Persistence
32. Nova	66. Vanity	
33. Cap	67. Notepad	

0. Lark	34. Adobe	68. Links
1. Dolt	35. Buffet	69. Semifinal
2. Homicide	36. Parameter	70. Bumper
3. Paganism	37. Crescent	71. Huckster
4. Fiction	38. Tee	72. Batten
5. Crossword	39. Lookout	73. Rodent
6. Flax	40. Typography	74. Plumb
7. Domicile	41. Earthquake	75. Pronoun
8. Operetta	42. Modesty	76. Moron
9. Duet	43. Lignite	77. Oaf
10. Refresh	44. Tortilla	78. Swan
11. Cobra	45. Pomegranate	79. Neatness
12. Infinitive	46. Hive	80. Launch
13. Republic	47. Surname	81. Impulse
14. Noon	48. Earth	82. Hideaway
15. Glossary	49. Libel	83. Genealogist
16. Soda	50. Nodule	84. Steer
17. Disk	51. Kilogram	85. Crochet
18. Uppercut	52. Bean	86. Samosa
19. Lizard	53. Furniture	87. Stag
20. Counterpoint	54. Wallaby	88. Inhospitality
21. Monastery	55. Impressionism	89. Bug
22. Paralysis	56. Toxicity	90. Caffeine
23. Dung	57. Acne	91. Residue
24. Icebreaker	58. Slaughter	92. Recruitment
25. Dissent	59. Residence	93. Train
26. Deprivation	60. Tomorrow	94. Corncob
27. Brewery	61. Trough	95. Dogma
28. Hell	62. Vet	96. Tunnel
29. Dependant	63. Gravel	97. Tendency
30. Inheritor	64. Sliver	98. Optician
31. Sportswear	65. Amber	99. Accent
32. Symphony	66. Janitor	
33. Dugout	67. Blob	

0. Loveliness	34. Sorrow	68. Things
1. Regret	35. Recital	69. Lacuna
2. Ermine	36. Heifer	70. Obstinacy
3. Lass	37. Grasp	71. Weather
4. Victim	38. Furlough	72. Heartland
5. Torment	39. Sideshow	73. Spruce
6. Kindling	40. Rig	74. Hallway
7. Stave	41. Scrooge	75. Cob
8. Fireplace	42. Porthole	76. Stout
9. Perversion	43. Holiday	77. Base
10. Slide	44. Ulema	78. Raider
11. Tuition	45. Screamer	79. Martin
12. Enchanter	46. Artisan	80. Sawfish
13. Sightseeing	47. Orderly	81. Recovery
14. Stardom	48. Scarab	82. Potential
15. Baker	49. Bunch	83. Backstroke
16. Reduction	50. Underpass	84. Pulp
17. Putter	51. Speculation	85. Disputation
18. Penchant	52. Crook	86. Stickball
19. Hall	53. Escapade	87. Maneuver
20. Rumpus	54. Kick	88. Evergreen
21. Litmus	55. Shred	89. Tent
22. Impression	56. Chemist	90. Baseball
23. Growth	57. Niche	91. Wheelchair
24. Misfortune	58. Optimist	92. Patrolman
25. Telegraph	59. Oasis	93. Robustness
26. Tightness	60. Troll	94. Appendix
27. Grill	61. Mercury	95. Compulsion
28. Lethargy	62. Nuisance	96. Sienna
29. Group	63. Globe	97. Undoing
30. Trowel	64. Tide	98. Mercenary
31. Platypus	65. Midnight	99. Fertilizer
32. Choice	66. Hoedown	
33. Minaret	67. Modulation	

0. Peninsula
1. Synagogue
2. Mourner
3. Storyboard
4. Grate
5. Umbrage
6. Destination
7. Wage
8. Felon
9. Theorem
10. Pestle
11. Sludge
12. Generator
13. Butcher
14. Adjuster
15. Scree
16. Wallpaper
17. Talc
18. Conduit
19. Crash
20. Divination
21. Militant
22. Dialog
23. Barometer
24. Joiner
25. Anaconda
26. Designer
27. Herald
28. Elbow
29. Groomsman
30. Aversion
31. Infantry
32. Nougat
33. Loyalist
34. Perpendicular
35. Fallout
36. Scorpion
37. Knitting
38. Bottleneck
39. Puppy
40. Sardine
41. Spray
42. Donkey
43. Homeroom
44. Hue
45. Peacock
46. Hype
47. Ploy
48. Protozoa
49. Bullet
50. Stork
51. Outburst
52. Housekeeping
53. Frosting
54. Pilot
55. Middle
56. Jihad
57. Administration
58. Vat
59. Tramcar
60. Medalist
61. Dump
62. Twin
63. Curve
64. Bear
65. Rebound
66. Toffee
67. Chariot
68. Girdle
69. Greed
70. Shock
71. Coward
72. Moonlight
73. Blood
74. Scuffle
75. Pair
76. Gain
77. Dissuasion
78. Weft
79. Index
80. Rib
81. Innards
82. Dossier
83. Esteem
84. Disinfectant
85. Magic
86. Incoherence
87. Shuffle
88. Hyacinth
89. Tablet
90. Portcullis
91. Librarian
92. Chestnut
93. Column
94. Sledgehammer
95. Rocket
96. Clothes
97. Lettering
98. Infamy
99. Dismissal

0. Steamroller
1. Dignitary
2. Scallion
3. Salute
4. Handgun
5. Baldness
6. Filth
7. Shower
8. Jumper
9. Worship
10. Protein
11. Gauze
12. Statuette
13. Paw
14. Rhetoric
15. Ram
16. Tweezers
17. Assignment
18. Counseling
19. Incitement
20. Twitter
21. Suction
22. Doom
23. Radio
24. Rail
25. Bugle
26. Gown
27. Fog
28. Postcard
29. Half
30. Hammock
31. Lavatory
32. Sauna
33. Satchel
34. Mutiny
35. Practice
36. Duty
37. Apiary
38. Honor
39. Regeneration
40. Letter
41. Glazier
42. Lullaby
43. Subjection
44. Parsley
45. Ringlet
46. Atheism
47. Photometer
48. Docket
49. Involvement
50. Plagiarism
51. Ten
52. Reason
53. Sextet
54. Bricklayer
55. Headhunter
56. Iguana
57. Scapegoat
58. Surgeon
59. Portal
60. Continence
61. Harpy
62. Picket
63. Culmination
64. Trophy
65. Province
66. Meridian
67. Insight
68. Brutality
69. Umbrella
70. Air
71. Serendipity
72. Democracy
73. Armada
74. Nod
75. Vendetta
76. Monoplane
77. Shawl
78. Molecule
79. Gymnastics
80. Missile
81. Medallion
82. Tidings
83. Association
84. Manner
85. Mute
86. Primary
87. Madness
88. Curtsy
89. Shop
90. August
91. Nave
92. Bulb
93. Expenditure
94. Watchdog
95. Music
96. Basement
97. Oversight
98. Baron
99. Muffler

0. Trolley	34. Nylon	68. Ventilation
1. Regalia	35. Conception	69. Quintet
2. Crock	36. Hostile	70. Refusal
3. Sombrero	37. Headlight	71. Undercarriage
4. Comedy	38. Walrus	72. Fawn
5. Aerobatics	39. Weir	73. Kimono
6. Bounty	40. Aristocrat	74. Reveler
7. Hacksaw	41. Spring	75. Ogress
8. Humorist	42. Sheaf	76. Astronomy
9. Wood	43. Takeover	77. Hour
10. Derivation	44. Conflict	78. Quiet
11. Frittata	45. Hindrance	79. Reverberation
12. Parkway	46. Intimidation	80. Bagpipes
13. Chimpanzee	47. Disbelief	81. Infomercial
14. Ward	48. Candy	82. Yelp
15. Mother	49. Fluster	83. Intonation
16. Sect	50. Lordship	84. Carpetbag
17. Foam	51. Trap	85. Drum
18. Pink	52. Loch	86. Bombshell
19. Draft	53. Jailer	87. Mule
20. Rat	54. Rook	88. Adulation
21. Munificence	55. Nonsense	89. Library
22. Seizure	56. Decoy	90. Concealment
23. Keep	57. Link	91. Outsider
24. Industry	58. Communicant	92. Chuckle
25. Scripture	59. Road	93. Inheritance
26. Zigzag	60. Leave	94. Inspiration
27. Backwoods	61. Bribe	95. Bacon
28. Championship	62. Always	96. Degeneracy
29. Crate	63. Condor	97. Pilgrim
30. Scoff	64. Antagonist	98. Pitchfork
31. Reflection	65. Darts	99. Berth
32. Hostess	66. Gazelle	
33. Yell	67. Haiku	

0. Churn	34. Interpreter	68. Manifest
1. Twaddle	35. Seesaw	69. Pinstripe
2. Effort	36. Retirement	70. Lease
3. Likelihood	37. Auction	71. Aerie
4. Throne	38. Feast	72. Expert
5. Trucker	39. Gravity	73. Lanolin
6. Editor	40. Decade	74. Bureau
7. Detention	41. Anchovy	75. Cheek
8. Foreigner	42. Pyrotechnics	76. Floorboard
9. Moonstone	43. Brevity	77. Sherbet
10. Blacksmith	44. Dragoon	78. Disposition
11. Resin	45. Countryside	79. Submersion
12. Opium	46. Rebate	80. Dromedary
13. Legume	47. Peppermint	81. Crest
14. Pacifier	48. Psychiatry	82. Grenade
15. Eon	49. Pixie	83. Humility
16. Rampage	50. Setback	84. Stupidity
17. Hillside	51. Squalor	85. Genus
18. Devotee	52. Volcano	86. Annotation
19. Palmistry	53. Locksmith	87. Apple
20. Liking	54. Symbol	88. Syllabus
21. Chest	55. Illusionist	89. Inaction
22. Jack	56. Ribbon	90. Loudspeaker
23. Edition	57. Style	91. Cabaret
24. Imprint	58. Cupcake	92. Heroism
25. Standard	59. Spelunking	93. Gyration
26. Interception	60. Pigpen	94. Spa
27. Physicist	61. Notch	95. Valedictorian
28. Hobby	62. Falsehood	96. Harp
29. Seat	63. Roundup	97. Timpani
30. Dwelling	64. Cargo	98. Prediction
31. Walk	65. Matting	99. Ruin
32. Street	66. Emphasis	
33. Satsuma	67. Mouse	

0. Clang	34. Hem	68. Clown
1. Civility	35. Overtime	69. Flippancy
2. Campus	36. Example	70. Unicycle
3. Circle	37. Psalmist	71. Necessity
4. Fitness	38. Seepage	72. Contortion
5. Brier	39. Cartridge	73. Custom
6. Pediment	40. Coral	74. Mall
7. Ash	41. Pistol	75. Reviewer
8. Buoyancy	42. Dipper	76. Pane
9. Mankind	43. Wallflower	77. Bumblebee
10. Allusion	44. Welterweight	78. Presentation
11. Malfunction	45. Velvet	79. Eyesight
12. Bandanna	46. Organ	80. Orphanage
13. Expectation	47. Disquiet	81. Vibrancy
14. Nitrogen	48. Omelet	82. Teetotaler
15. Congestion	49. Stop	83. Vegetable
16. Carriage	50. Geyser	84. Ambler
17. Patch	51. Zoology	85. Southeast
18. Medal	52. Repugnance	86. Duchess
19. Amulet	53. Farce	87. Disruption
20. Penetration	54. Nature	88. Feet
21. Rutabaga	55. Importance	89. Impurity
22. Interlude	56. Storyteller	90. Musketeer
23. Windsurfing	57. Poetess	91. Quadrille
24. Reconciliation	58. Resemblance	92. Daffodil
25. Trip	59. Vocation	93. Rummage
26. Utensil	60. Lounger	94. Premiere
27. Electricity	61. Sachet	95. Solubility
28. Rind	62. Stroll	96. Ebb
29. Snapdragon	63. Fritter	97. Kennel
30. Multiple	64. Offense	98. Mold
31. Cosmetic	65. Stairwell	99. Arctic
32. Menace	66. Exposition	
33. Butchery	67. Bodyguard	

0. Slate
1. Swoon
2. Pentagon
3. Priority
4. North
5. Topics
6. Introvert
7. Reservation
8. Sewerage
9. Intern
10. Dreamer
11. Doomsday
12. Shareholder
13. Titanium
14. Harm
15. Lineage
16. Stickler
17. Quantity
18. Clause
19. Permission
20. Kid
21. Writ
22. Abbess
23. Blaze
24. Priestess
25. Poop
26. Purchaser
27. Hen
28. Seam
29. Hierarchy
30. Sprain
31. Garter
32. Oyster
33. Sophistication
34. Hospitalization
35. Maharajah
36. Jig
37. Heather
38. Household
39. Ambition
40. Mop
41. Pizza
42. Footnote
43. Pendant
44. Match
45. January
46. Decorator
47. Converse
48. Theater
49. Ruthlessness
50. Homestead
51. Cauldron
52. Dash
53. Tray
54. Dabbler
55. Potash
56. Monk
57. Spire
58. Interim
59. Howl
60. Leaf
61. Debris
62. Bin
63. Haversack
64. Penguin
65. Stabilizer
66. Gait
67. Vegan
68. Beggar
69. Newspaper
70. Bandage
71. Misquotation
72. Seller
73. Pamphlet
74. Volunteer
75. Archives
76. Limbo
77. Interjection
78. Bogie
79. Contrariety
80. Down
81. Bearer
82. Woodwork
83. Monsoon
84. Smash
85. Courtship
86. Needlepoint
87. Tripod
88. Chaotic
89. Flare
90. Shrimp
91. Marmot
92. Scum
93. Shipbuilding
94. Asparagus
95. Antibiotic
96. Longevity
97. Cutlass
98. Rectification
99. Ambiguity

0. Vogue
1. Preamble
2. Applause
3. Access
4. Aggressor
5. Pilgrimage
6. Tempter
7. Density
8. Cohesion
9. Exodus
10. Sac
11. Renunciation
12. Disreputable
13. Laziness
14. Pupil
15. Stagecoach
16. Boon
17. Range
18. Truss
19. Dislike
20. Tenement
21. Alcohol
22. Report
23. Chocolate
24. Orthodontist
25. Comb
26. Siege
27. Hypnosis
28. Warfare
29. Sieve
30. Sari
31. Switchboard
32. Quiver
33. Waffle
34. Madam
35. Shirt
36. Prophecy
37. Absentee
38. Fuchsia
39. Stand
40. Crossing
41. Bacteria
42. Parrot
43. Dais
44. Face
45. Mechanism
46. Blouse
47. Treble
48. Molding
49. Madcap
50. Beer
51. Maniac
52. Rareness
53. Whippoorwill
54. Breach
55. Toxin
56. Tincture
57. Cornflower
58. Tumbleweed
59. Carton
60. System
61. Overdraft
62. Village
63. Chivalry
64. Clumsiness
65. Silkworm
66. Feasibility
67. Nucleus
68. Adoption
69. Longitude
70. Violin
71. Kopek
72. Mole
73. Son
74. Following
75. Plus
76. Forceps
77. Telephone
78. Servant
79. Transplant
80. Breaker
81. Splinter
82. Immoralism
83. Whorl
84. Growl
85. Fumigation
86. Equipment
87. Etiquette
88. Foil
89. Clique
90. Lure
91. Stint
92. Twirl
93. Sprinkling
94. Sandpiper
95. Savage
96. Recognition
97. Homage
98. Dismay
99. Lucidity

0. Geranium	34. Smell	68. Desire
1. Jasper	35. Gush	69. Sleight
2. Fault	36. Hemisphere	70. Ignorance
3. Musician	37. Shantytown	71. Nunnery
4. Blink	38. Remark	72. Inaccuracy
5. Casualty	39. Buff	73. Imbecile
6. Creeper	40. Purr	74. Salad
7. Chime	41. Stamen	75. Utopia
8. Ditty	42. Pagan	76. Drunkard
9. Plateau	43. Slacker	77. Humanist
10. Snipe	44. Surroundings	78. Occupant
11. Hair	45. Contravention	79. Turpentine
12. Mama	46. Saying	80. Hatchet
13. Alabaster	47. Flexibility	81. Sacrilege
14. Hovel	48. Trapper	82. Corroboration
15. Usury	49. Cablegram	83. Thermostat
16. Spite	50. Spank	84. Mite
17. Crusade	51. Course	85. Shove
18. Sublet	52. Tourism	86. Nana
19. Combat	53. Granary	87. Fundamentalism
20. Suitcase	54. Breed	88. Slime
21. Vestment	55. Bullion	89. Aviator
22. Handsel	56. Hemlock	90. Trappings
23. Courtyard	57. Steamer	91. Realism
24. Spelling	58. Plumbing	92. Arsenal
25. Servitude	59. Analyst	93. Discoverer
26. Marionette	60. Sincerity	94. Bonnet
27. Signal	61. Emu	95. Horsepower
28. Colonnade	62. Violator	96. Culprit
29. Narcissist	63. Cross	97. Ax
30. Upstart	64. Feta	98. Sisterhood
31. Nerd	65. Shipwreck	99. Locket
32. Rumor	66. Fold	
33. Economics	67. Northeast	

0. Mouthful
1. Feature
2. Mountain
3. Garlic
4. Matador
5. Moment
6. Opponent
7. Docility
8. Welter
9. Sushi
10. Struggle
11. Cannonball
12. Web
13. Candidate
14. Hermit
15. Smack
16. News
17. Perpetration
18. Nightclub
19. Trial
20. Electrode
21. Monarchist
22. Paintbrush
23. Congress
24. Sunrise
25. Confidence
26. Iris
27. Bias
28. Operative
29. Madman
30. Crone
31. Physician
32. Foliage
33. Bowline

34. Graze
35. Rate
36. Mast
37. Posture
38. Heckler
39. Maid
40. Mug
41. Butter
42. Hypotenuse
43. Napkin
44. Ken
45. Masterpiece
46. Zucchini
47. Lodge
48. Straggler
49. Chalk
50. Captivity
51. Torch
52. Suspicion
53. Empress
54. Cistern
55. Parenthesis
56. Excise
57. Output
58. Vampire
59. Symbolism
60. Irritant
61. Blasphemy
62. Denim
63. Wife
64. Communication
65. Sameness
66. Wastage
67. Sack

68. Emission
69. Utterance
70. Bakery
71. Furor
72. Formula
73. Jackal
74. Notebook
75. Mystic
76. Prince
77. Robbery
78. Misrule
79. Bet
80. Falcon
81. Warning
82. Conclusion
83. Hoof
84. Man
85. Gospel
86. Partnership
87. Conviction
88. Radiance
89. Awe
90. Repayment
91. Fortitude
92. Fair
93. Ravine
94. Adviser
95. Greens
96. Plywood
97. Orthopedics
98. Weapon
99. Process

0. Purchase	34. Engagement	68. Deli
1. Agony	35. Supervision	69. Manufacture
2. Engine	36. Butterfly	70. Apathy
3. Paraffin	37. Urchin	71. Log
4. Coolness	38. Meaning	72. Crime
5. Sponsor	39. Pestilence	73. Mackerel
6. Certificate	40. Wench	74. Choke
7. Relevancy	41. Luminary	75. Supremacy
8. November	42. Notification	76. Sitting
9. Cribbage	43. Whip	77. Slot
10. Tack	44. Kirk	78. Patrol
11. Parabola	45. Hardware	79. Louse
12. Height	46. Ignition	80. Fell
13. Stage	47. Cocaine	81. Toothpaste
14. Cult	48. Puffin	82. Neigh
15. Spoilsport	49. Stability	83. Gaze
16. Dosage	50. Treatise	84. Deserts
17. Suspect	51. Push	85. Play
18. Snowfall	52. Galley	86. Rap
19. Baritone	53. Float	87. Improvisation
20. Gerbil	54. Inexactitude	88. Handout
21. Machinery	55. September	89. Coma
22. Resolution	56. Autograph	90. Fantail
23. Wrong	57. Thesaurus	91. Harpoon
24. Fad	58. Couch	92. Desktop
25. Scamp	59. Society	93. Suck
26. Rosary	60. Servility	94. Reservoir
27. Quarrel	61. Calfskin	95. Operation
28. Friendliness	62. Octave	96. Rifle
29. Track	63. Flatfish	97. Consolation
30. Crudity	64. Hazelnut	98. Duck
31. Sneak	65. Reaction	99. Hip
32. Sheep	66. Kernel	
33. Undercoating	67. Sorceress	

0. Attack
1. Debtor
2. Reminiscence
3. Skip
4. Rigging
5. Garbage
6. Frolic
7. Ion
8. Valuer
9. Length
10. Starch
11. Geography
12. Bone
13. Lectern
14. Skink
15. Streak
16. Rocker
17. Paddock
18. Slush
19. Travel
20. Production
21. Custody
22. Category
23. Capture
24. Situation
25. Stile
26. Laughter
27. Variable
28. Shipper
29. Antibody
30. Mediocrity
31. Cuisine
32. Tease
33. Package
34. Occupancy
35. Pontiff
36. Assistant
37. Deduction
38. Flicker
39. Probation
40. Prisoner
41. Facility
42. Telephonist
43. Pathway
44. Stoneware
45. Hullabaloo
46. Dockyard
47. Boa
48. Ownership
49. Unison
50. Kipper
51. Villainy
52. Porridge
53. Shutter
54. Adventurer
55. Catholic
56. Quittance
57. Sophomore
58. Threshold
59. Typographer
60. Terseness
61. Gratification
62. Rerun
63. Hexagram
64. Digit
65. Fare
66. Misdirection
67. Crumb
68. Daze
69. Marsupial
70. Gnu
71. Motive
72. Enlistment
73. Wringer
74. Petrel
75. Cough
76. Eloquence
77. Quintuplet
78. Plumage
79. Inefficiency
80. Builder
81. Foundry
82. Gym
83. Elite
84. Armlet
85. Affability
86. Clap
87. Diplomatic
88. Ballot
89. Doubt
90. Bristle
91. Worm
92. Neurologist
93. Imitator
94. Majority
95. Briskness
96. Emporium
97. Consensus
98. Keel
99. Sideboard

0. Treadmill	34. Tribute	68. Rake
1. Cooper	35. Prejudice	69. Deadline
2. Wolf	36. Equation	70. Whirlpool
3. Kilt	37. Libretto	71. Present
4. Assessor	38. Bombardment	72. Prod
5. Inequality	39. Trait	73. Magnetism
6. Mastermind	40. Disappearance	74. Veil
7. Step	41. Diplomat	75. Quality
8. Jujitsu	42. Bowler	76. Waif
9. Stimulant	43. Antique	77. Ultimatum
10. Drawback	44. Lollipop	78. Number
11. Benevolence	45. Crossbreed	79. Jupiter
12. Ostrich	46. Hew	80. Knickers
13. Cruet	47. Straw	81. Chat
14. Mom	48. Particle	82. Imp
15. Partner	49. Adversary	83. Distress
16. Bangle	50. Imminence	84. Deadliness
17. Plumber	51. Populace	85. Frame
18. Founder	52. Prominence	86. Canister
19. Maidenhood	53. Connoisseur	87. Grime
20. Sedan	54. Solstice	88. Masque
21. Stomp	55. Saw	89. Coop
22. Obliteration	56. Calligraphy	90. Ability
23. Prom	57. Breeches	91. Liaison
24. Pathos	58. Futility	92. Toot
25. Bogey	59. Juice	93. Airplane
26. Housefly	60. Confection	94. Greenhouse
27. Fury	61. Salesmanship	95. Springtime
28. Commonplace	62. Keyboard	96. Dishonesty
29. Jade	63. Manager	97. Cigar
30. Jog	64. Undertaking	98. Contortionist
31. Shrouds	65. Corporal	99. Increase
32. Spirituality	66. Anguish	
33. Dizziness	67. Schoolbook	

0. Doodle	34. Barrier	68. Card
1. Lacrosse	35. Traction	69. Ration
2. Scene	36. Sociology	70. Design
3. Passage	37. Montage	71. Liquid
4. Watercolor	38. Pollination	72. Zephyr
5. Cookie	39. Color	73. Viscount
6. Harness	40. Science	74. Updraft
7. Interior	41. Cascade	75. Planner
8. Weekday	42. Chloride	76. Translation
9. Poplar	43. Squawk	77. Thoughtfulness
10. Oregano	44. Mantelpiece	78. Brunt
11. Potentiality	45. Vantage	79. Perfumer
12. Fingering	46. Quote	80. Camcorder
13. Roof	47. Pluto	81. Toll
14. Mannerism	48. Profile	82. Jar
15. Hash	49. Dread	83. Path
16. Stigma	50. Glass	84. Pessimist
17. Rock	51. Dude	85. Raise
18. Palace	52. Investor	86. Official
19. Corporation	53. Collards	87. Wail
20. Misadventure	54. Sonneteer	88. Instance
21. Godson	55. Relation	89. Angling
22. Wear	56. Fastness	90. Flank
23. Coin	57. Slipcover	91. Decline
24. Hypocrite	58. Cougar	92. Fight
25. Washer	59. Incubator	93. Deal
26. Vein	60. Airship	94. Huntsman
27. Squid	61. Disparagement	95. Leather
28. Pliers	62. Captive	96. Puzzle
29. Ridicule	63. Sawdust	97. Cumulus
30. Molasses	64. Stool	98. Freelancer
31. Bookkeeping	65. Idol	99. Dinginess
32. Aptness	66. Spill	
33. Sentiment	67. Medley	

0. Mauve	34. Inducement	68. Manicurist
1. Vandal	35. Florist	69. Flask
2. Dogfish	36. Heretic	70. Guidebook
3. Dissertation	37. Lodestar	71. Glade
4. Spokesman	38. Grocer	72. Superman
5. Speedwell	39. Propriety	73. Thirst
6. Registry	40. Biennial	74. Chatter
7. Parka	41. Parlor	75. Morn
8. Denial	42. Golf	76. Retreat
9. Escort	43. Ninth	77. Insider
10. Tot	44. Cafeteria	78. Task
11. Pollutant	45. Pittance	79. Divorce
12. Feminism	46. Minor	80. Latitude
13. Hum	47. Rebel	81. Donation
14. Appendage	48. Chum	82. Swatch
15. Forensic	49. Microphone	83. Carousal
16. Thrill	50. Stadium	84. Defect
17. Teacher	51. Patron	85. Conceit
18. Grouse	52. Splutter	86. Physique
19. Viability	53. Playground	87. Optics
20. Miracle	54. Upland	88. Lubricator
21. Goods	55. Immensity	89. Exaggeration
22. Jingle	56. Moan	90. Centralization
23. Adept	57. Medicine	91. Chipmunk
24. Survey	58. Cutting	92. Plating
25. Sheet	59. Lot	93. Hacienda
26. Buoy	60. Commotion	94. Craftsman
27. Sequel	61. Caterpillar	95. Malignancy
28. Twenty	62. Honeymoon	96. Opening
29. Repulsion	63. Flashlight	97. Coarseness
30. Forge	64. Journalist	98. Perdition
31. Sofa	65. Button	99. Grating
32. Journalism	66. Airline	
33. Sabotage	67. Payroll	

0. Surgery	34. Plow	68. Taboo
1. Liveliness	35. Appropriation	69. Deformity
2. Lieutenant	36. Flea	70. Stalagmite
3. Multiplication	37. Debate	71. Alliteration
4. Xenophobia	38. Matron	72. Sickle
5. Rivulet	39. Tub	73. Discourse
6. Show	40. Ineffectiveness	74. Trance
7. Menu	41. Run	75. Polyester
8. Salt	42. Tribesman	76. Transformer
9. Videotape	43. Skullcap	77. Sandman
10. Dance	44. Cleft	78. Lobelia
11. Mood	45. Beginner	79. Gully
12. Jockey	46. Privatization	80. Dependence
13. Spool	47. Gaudiness	81. Waiter
14. Myriad	48. Pesticide	82. Triathlon
15. Wraith	49. Language	83. Screw
16. Discoloration	50. Conglomerate	84. Misconception
17. Lamp	51. Ivory	85. Poltergeist
18. Nakedness	52. Creak	86. Hod
19. Iota	53. Therapist	87. Shrine
20. Turquoise	54. Plumpness	88. Sage
21. Millstone	55. Academy	89. Cadet
22. Plunge	56. Downpour	90. Snob
23. Avoidance	57. Arch	91. Crypt
24. Crocodile	58. Dish	92. Ornithology
25. Misnomer	59. Arrival	93. Fungus
26. Basket	60. Slug	94. Tanker
27. Pope	61. Slacks	95. Foreboding
28. Gravy	62. Banister	96. Finale
29. Petition	63. Overhaul	97. Durability
30. Laptop	64. Analysis	98. Solvent
31. Correctness	65. Hawthorn	99. Bruise
32. Underpants	66. Magazine	
33. Boudoir	67. Plantation	

0. Encouragement	34. Forgery	68. Dart
1. Expedition	35. Ground	69. Clef
2. Dividend	36. Signatory	70. Precinct
3. Chapter	37. Vision	71. Collapse
4. Cook	38. Bundle	72. Hibiscus
5. Gong	39. Arbiter	73. Refrigerator
6. Creamery	40. Measure	74. Beaver
7. Narrows	41. Adder	75. Deluge
8. Army	42. Prattle	76. Poker
9. Yellow	43. Factory	77. Conclude
10. Malt	44. Symmetry	78. Release
11. Literature	45. Variance	79. Officer
12. Surveyor	46. Portfolio	80. Perusal
13. Joist	47. Severance	81. Fine
14. Tram	48. Conversion	82. Gnat
15. Ebony	49. Shame	83. Screenwriter
16. Ambush	50. Brigadier	84. Convener
17. God	51. Melody	85. Creek
18. Head	52. Overflow	86. Scarp
19. Posse	53. Corner	87. Premium
20. Nanny	54. Sharpie	88. Wren
21. Sex	55. Darling	89. Consideration
22. Dip	56. Prison	90. Beetroot
23. Skillet	57. Icebox	91. Commission
24. Stone	58. Tonic	92. Ornament
25. Drawbridge	59. Vivacity	93. Concern
26. Woodchuck	60. Cooperative	94. Mulberry
27. Peer	61. Mint	95. Cockerel
28. Jerky	62. Tractor	96. Momentum
29. Roadrunner	63. Wrench	97. Sandlot
30. Ladle	64. Braid	98. Hat
31. Tubing	65. Penalty	99. Curtain
32. Paraphrase	66. Billow	
33. Incompatibility	67. Swab	

0. Doctor	34. Knoll	68. Pad
1. Runaway	35. Maintenance	69. Alias
2. Hatchback	36. Ogre	70. Relapse
3. Surliness	37. Trout	71. Glove
4. Suppliant	38. Dirge	72. Stub
5. Carburetor	39. Jiffy	73. Calf
6. Handshake	40. Eve	74. Lemonade
7. Bagel	41. Trump	75. Vote
8. Ignoramus	42. Cigarette	76. Catastrophe
9. Philosophy	43. Fabric	77. Girder
10. Competition	44. Applicant	78. House
11. Bulletin	45. Infant	79. Detonation
12. Incompetency	46. Precision	80. Holder
13. Hunger	47. Sunshine	81. Genealogy
14. Handcuffs	48. Homework	82. Hovercraft
15. Cylinder	49. Desirability	83. Separatism
16. Marketing	50. Laugh	84. Albatross
17. Bibliography	51. Delay	85. Sander
18. Mitigation	52. Gingerbread	86. Nutrient
19. Jumble	53. Earmuffs	87. Mirror
20. Flow	54. Concurrence	88. Flotsam
21. Sandstone	55. Prop	89. Script
22. Draper	56. Spur	90. Trudge
23. Huipil	57. Sneaker	91. Outlet
24. Fourth	58. Tin	92. Explosive
25. Embers	59. Instruction	93. Housewife
26. Ton	60. Anemone	94. Problem
27. Miscreant	61. Survivor	95. Silhouette
28. Charity	62. Powerhouse	96. Gage
29. Dowager	63. Ideal	97. Realization
30. Forgetfulness	64. Carafe	98. Encirclement
31. Plank	65. Jute	99. Superintendent
32. Misprint	66. Fluency	
33. Tarragon	67. Sickbed